PEG L

C0-GCE-934

MUSICAL STRUCTURE AND DESIGN

CEDRIC THORPE DAVIE
A.R.C.M.
*Head of Music Department,
University of St. Andrews*

DOVER PUBLICATIONS, INC.
NEW YORK

All rights reserved under Pan American and International Copyright Conventions.

This Dover edition, first published in 1966, is an unabridged and unaltered republication of the work originally published by Dennis Dobson in 1953.

This edition is published by special arrangement with Dobson Books, Ltd., 80 Kensington Church Street, London W. 8, England.

International Standard Book Number: 0-486-21629-2
Library of Congress Catalog Card Number: 66-20421

Manufactured in the United States of America

Dover Publications, Inc.
180 Varick Street
New York, N. Y. 10014

CONTENTS

FOREWORD

ONE WOULD BE tempted to describe Mr Thorpe Davie (after the conventional manner) as a rising young composer, were it not for the fact that he has risen. His music for three celebrated plays at the Edinburgh Festival—*The Three Estates, The Gentle Shepherd* and *The Highland Fair*—for the Stratford productions of *Henry VIII* and *King Lear*, as well as other works, has won not only respect but affection. The reason is, of course, that Mr Thorpe Davie knows precisely how best to set out his music so that it may be intelligible. His musical aim, for which he is much in our gratitude, is clarity and not obscurity. We may suspect that his Scottish antecedents have had something to do with this. At any rate Scotland is confident that opinion which places him among the leaders of Scottish art represents enlightenment.

Clearly the structure and design of music is a musician's business. The creative artist knows so much more about it than the pedant or (dare we say?) the critic. The difficulty is that few composers are happy in literary expression. This one is an exception.

Therefore the student may turn to this work with confidence. He will find that much stock-in-trade information on 'form' is composed of *non sequiturs* which, in turn, originate in fallacies. The emotional background to sonata, the relation—as in the concerto—between habits of performance and musical style, the qualities of Haydn, Mozart and Purcell (in particular), the necessity for analysis by ear rather than by eye; these are some of the matters to receive treatment which can only stimulate the reader. So much music is critically reviewed that no one who has read this work with care will feel ill at ease in regard to the design of music.

Tovey is often quoted herein. The Tovey addict will find Mr Thorpe Davie congenial company. He will recognise much that Tovey did say and much that Tovey did not say. In short this book goes forward, even though in some respects it is bound to go backward P.M.Y.

INTRODUCTION

EVER SINCE THERE have been men who have deliberately set out to compose pieces of music, and to give them a more or less permanent form by recording them in writing, they have been faced with one problem above all others. That problem arises at some point during the progress of the composition, and stated baldly, it takes the form of the question 'What shall I do next?'

In some periods of musical history, various different satisfactory kinds of solution have been found. At other times, composers have been less sure of themselves. Indeed, practically the whole of one century—the seventeenth—was devoted to the task of evolving, by the trial-and-error method, suitable ways of achieving continuity in that music employing instruments which (following on the invention and development of the violin family), replaced the hitherto prevailing purely vocal forms just about the end of the sixteenth century. Not that the composers of that day were conscious of being primarily concerned with any such thing; musical history shows that deliberate preoccupation with externals cannot of itself result in the production of masterpieces.

The aim of this book is to describe the answers which the best composers of different periods have given to the above question; to discuss the varying structural requirements of different musical styles, and to illustrate from the music itself the ways in which the greatest musical creative artists have met these requirements.

The most casual lover of music will find greater enjoyment in his listening if he has some understanding of the long- and short-range plans of the composer, for without it music can be only a matter of the momentary enjoyment of isolated sensations which happen to reach the seat of the emotions. To the serious music-student, whether he be an aspirant to the profession of music, or a listener determined to extract from the art as much as he can of that which so many great men have put into it, intimate and conscious understanding of design is even more important than close acquaintance with the technical details of harmony and counterpoint. For the composer, appreciation of the methods and achievements of his forerunners is the only sure foundation upon which he can build for himself.

To hear music and to listen to it are not necessarily the same thing. One can *hear* while thinking about something else, just as one can see things from the window of a bus while the attention is elsewhere; but *listening* requires continuous attention to the music, as a play requires continuous attention to the words and action.

Attentive listening is for several reasons much more widespread today than it was, say, fifty years ago. There is a more general understanding of the fact that great music is not something that has come into being, as it were by magic, through an intermediary known as a composer, but that it is the careful, thoughtful, and largely deliberate creation of men whose aptitude, inclination, studies and labour have all been concentrated on the creation of something which did not exist before. This realisation has led to an increase in the number of listeners who have found pleasure in doing justice to the creators of these new things by giving their work the close attention which it deserves.

This word 'attention' is really the key to the whole matter. It is no very formidable task to devote one's mental energy for a short time to concentration upon the unfolding design of a piece of music, any more than it is to read a book; indeed, there are many similarities between attentive listening and attentive reading, and the student of music would do well to regard his listening as an occupation calling upon much the same faculties as his reading. The one essential *difference* lies in the need, in attentive listening, for exercising the memory to the extent of being able to recognise the re-appearance of passages already heard; but the development of this faculty is by no means difficult, and it is quickly improved by practice and experience. There is no need for alarm at early failures to recollect certain features of music that have been heard; ability to do so grows quickly, and is helped by the repeated hearings of the same piece which the gramophone makes possible.

The understanding, and therefore the study, of musical design (or form, or structure), is one of the essentials of intelligent attentive listening; but it brings with it a very real danger which the examination system, and the text-books written with that system in view, have tended to accentuate.

The author's experience has been, (great as is the number of books devoted in whole or in part to the subject of musical design, and excellent as is the quality of some of them), that too little stress is as a rule laid upon the fact that music is an art which includes time (measured in hours, minutes and seconds) among its elements; in other words, that it exists not on paper to be looked at, but *in the time element to be listened to*; that the printed copy is no more than a series of reminders or indications of what the music is intended to *sound* like, and that no amount of paper ingenuity is of the slightest consequence, or is even related to the art of music at all, unless it signifies an effect which can be appreciated *by the ear*. This book contains several reminders of the need for regarding music as matter for appreciation through actual hearing, and the author makes no apology for the fact, since the book has failed in its purpose if it does not do something to remedy this defect of some of its predecessors.

It is useless to imagine that by examining the printed copy and marking off sections of the music as if they were measurable in feet and inches, one can acquire much idea of the really important aspects of musical design. It would be easy to take all the sonata-movements that Beethoven ever wrote, and measure them off in this way. One would probably receive the impression that the master had produced some hundreds of almost identical objects, and might be forgiven for wondering why Beethoven should be regarded as the intellectual superior of anybody working on a mass-production line.

Teachers and students alike run the risk, if they are not ever watchful of the need to regard music *as music,* of confusing the basic design with the finished individual product; of coming—to put the point slightly differently—to regard musical forms as if they were moulds into which composers simply have to pour their music; or (a better simile) as if they were like architects' plans to which unlimited numbers of virtually identical houses may be constructed.

The truth about musical design is far different, and may well be illustrated by reference rather to living beings. For example, no two humans are quite alike in appearance, let alone in spirit and character; the same can be said of cats or dogs, and no doubt of earwigs or cheese-mites. Yet all the members of each species conform to a common type, in so far as all are built on a recognisably similar framework, while all have common outward characteristics (e.g., all humans have two eyes, ten toes, and so on). Similarly, no two pieces of music are exactly alike. Each piece has its own unique characteristics and personality, evolved from its own materials and in its own environment. Yet the progress of the art of music has brought with it the evolution of a number of well-defined types of structural basis, to one or another of which the majority of movements conform.

In this sense, there can be said to exist an *anatomy* of music, and the profitable study of musical design consists in *mastering the anatomical principles without losing sight of the fact that they are no more than that,* and then examining the ways in which the great composers have made them the basis of the living individual organisms which are their creations.

This book claims to be a text-book only in so far as it may help to clarify the practice of the great men of the past; it does not pretend to give information as to how the music of the present should be designed, since the author is convinced that great music exists only where significant musical material is allied to the form which *for itself* is the right one, and that a large percentage of the music of today (as of every age) will be found by posterity not to meet this condition, and will be discarded as the concertos of Hummel have been discarded, no matter how interesting it may be to its composers' contemporaries. Let the composer, therefore, work out his own salvation; if he is a great man with important things to say, he will learn how to say them in the best way, as Bach, Mozart, and Wagner did.

It is dangerous to rely too much upon analogy, but we may helpfully compare the position of the composer producing living pieces of music—each with its own individuality yet belonging to its species—with that of the great classical painters, whose intimate knowledge of anatomy provided the basis upon which they created their figures, giving them life and character by their genius. The music-student, whether he would write music, or understand fully what others have written, must learn his musical anatomy; but, having mastered it, he must beware of any temptation to regard pieces of music which he cannot fit to preconceived notions of 'form' as being defective in design.

Sir Donald Tovey writing of Beethoven's pianoforte sonata in B flat (op. 22), says that it 'is the work in which Beethoven has achieved as pure a normality as an art-form can maintain without losing its individual life'.[1] Elsewhere he calls the same piece 'the most conventional of all Beethoven's works'[2] and 'Beethoven's one model sonata.'[3] This is as much as to say that, while it is possible, by taking the average measurements of all human beings, to produce a mathematical statement of the size, weight, features and character of a theoretical 'average man', such men do not in fact exist; or, if one can be found, he is just as much an individual, different from all other individuals, as any one of the other two

[1] *Companion to Beethoven's pianoforte sonatas,* p. 86.
[2] *Beethoven,* p. 106.
[3] *Collected Articles from the* Encyclopædia Britannica, p. 125.

thousand million human beings who are not 'average'. Similarly, some movements (for example, the first movement of Mozart's pianoforte concerto in A major, K. 488) may coincide in most respects with the average proportions of all examples; but they are not for that reason necessarily either more or less perfect than other pieces.

Human beings are interesting according to the beauty of appearance and individuality of character which they develop on their own account out of their share of the common material, rather than because of the number of their ribs. Similarly, pieces of music are interesting when they bring variety and originality of thought to the basic designs.

As a consequence of the need to keep within reasonable limits of space, the anatomical principles which underly the Western European music of the three-and-a-half centuries between 1550 and 1900 are set forth in this book somewhat baldly. For the student who wishes to go more closely into the theory of the matter, a short bibliography of some of the most rewarding books has been provided. More space is thereby made available for discussion of the real music which the great composers have given us, not by breathing life into dead bodies, but by bringing about the growth of living ones.

Many of the illustrations in this book consist of detailed analyses of certain pieces of music which can only be appreciated by close reference to the printed copy in preparation for, and in conjunction with, actual aural acquaintance; a relatively simple matter for the student of today who has gramophone and radio at his disposal. The author's aim has been to use for the illustrations such music as is easily accessible either by purchase or in good public libraries, and (where it cannot be played for study purposes by a pianist of average ability) is frequently to be heard by wireless, or easily obtainable in recorded form.

It remains to take note of three indispensible conditions for the successful study of musical design. The first is, that the student must regard text-books, including the present one, as no more than aids to his unceasing study of the music itself. [Such study need never come to an end within the span of one human life, and provided it is always directed towards music as *heard* and not as looked at in print, it will always be rewarded by an ever-increasing insight into the workings of great minds, and by continuous satisfaction in and enjoyment of their work.]

The second condition is, that the student must take note of the revolution brought about in the understanding of music by the writings of Sir Donald Tovey, and be prepared to draw upon them constantly for help and guidance in his own work. It is no exaggeration to say that no printed word of Tovey's can safely be ignored by anyone who takes music seriously; but, above all, his volume of *Musical Articles from the Encyclopaedia Britannica,* his *Beethoven* and his seven volumes of *Essays in Musical Analysis* should be the constant companion of the student.

The third condition is set out by the late Dr R. O. Morris in his book *The Structure of Music,* where he insists upon the need for the student to build up at least a small library of basic musical texts for himself. The actual possession, for immediate and constant reference, of such things as Beethoven's pianoforte sonatas, Bach's '48', and miniature scores of a few dozen of the greatest things in choral, orchestral and chamber music is essential. Even in these hard days there are many rewards for the diligent searcher of second-hand music-shops and catalogues, and some shillings (or pounds) spent upon scores as occasion and ability allow, constitute a real investment just as certainly as the money spent by a joiner upon his tools.

The glossary of musical forms claims only to give a few essential facts, and should be supplemented where necessary by reference to *Grove's Dictionary.*

I

THE SMALLEST UNITS OF MUSICAL DESIGN

THE CONSTRUCTION OF intelligible music is akin in many respects to that of intelligible verse or prose. Musical sounds, like words, are built into clauses, sentences and paragraphs; and big movements, like the chapters of a novel or the cantos of an epic poem, are constructed of successions of logically-connected paragraphs.

Also, as literature is punctuated by commas, colons, full stops and the rest, so is music punctuated continuously by the chord-progressions known as cadences. It is taken for granted that the student is familiar with the sound of the most frequently-used cadences, but it is necessary to say a few words about them at this point. Cadences fall into three broad classes—those which give the mental impressions of rest, of incompleteness, and of surprise. The first class includes perfect and plagal cadences; the second imperfect, and the third interrupted cadences. But within each class there is a very large scope for subtlety of grading; compare, for example, the effects of two perfect cadences, in the first of which the melody comes to rest on the mediant, and in the second on the tonic.

Ex. 1

It needs no particular sensitivity of ear to recognise that though both give the impression of *rest,* the second cadence of the example has a much greater feeling of finality. So it is within the other groups; for instance, the mild surprise of the frequently-used interrupted cadence formed by the move from dominant to submediant harmony (ex. 2a) may be compared with the sudden, shattering, explosion in Chopin's *Fantaisie* (ex. 2b).

Ex. 2a

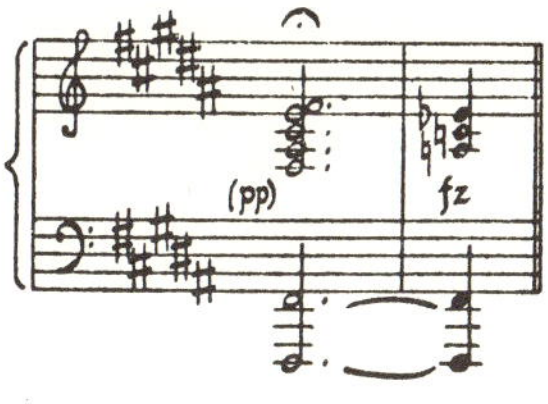

Ex. 2b

In addition, there is the cross-bred type of cadence formed by using inverted positions of perfect or plagal cadences, the mental effect of which may be akin to a mild full close (ex. 3a) or to a half-close (ex. 3b).

Schubert: Impromptu in Ab. Op 142 no 2.

Ex. 3a

Mozart: Symphony No. 41.

Ex. 3b

The smallest rhythmic unit with which we need be concerned is the *phrase,* the musical counterpart of the literary clause.[4] While it is a matter of some difficulty to give a verbal definition of a 'phrase' which will convey anything of its meaning as a *musical* entity, there is no difficulty at all about listening to a hymn-tune or a folk-tune and realising by ear the natural 'breathing points' at which such a tune breaks its absolute continuity. Each such breathing point is a cadence, and *each cadence marks the end of a phrase,* which is thus seen to be a unit of a few bars, ending with a cadence of some kind, and having a certain unity of its own, quite often (but by no means always) shown by a gradual movement to a

[4] Many phrases can be subdivided into two or more *sections,* and may be made up of the repeated use of still smaller 'figures', whose individuality of rhythm or melodic contour may determine the whole character of the piece.

climax about two-thirds of the way from its start, followed by a subsidence to the cadence. Phrases vary in length from 3 to 6 bars—smaller and larger ones are occasionally found, but are rare. The 4-bar phrase is by far the commonest, and has even been called the 'normal' phrase by many respectable writers; but the implication that the 3- and 5-bar phrases which litter the works of Purcell, Haydn and Brahms are in any way abnormal cannot be accepted, and the most we can admit is that the regularity of the 4-bar phrase, and the ease with which it may be mentally divided into halves and quarters, make it the most readily acceptable to that human instinct for regular recurrent accent which Tovey calls 'body-rhythm'.

The student should study carefully the following examples of phrases of different lengths, singing and playing them to himself till he is sure that he can feel their essential quality as musical *units,* and concentrating in particular upon the cadence. He should then do likewise with as many as he possibly can of the list which follows. Some time spent in this way will be well repaid.

3-bar phrases from Mozart's Symphony No. 40.

Ex. 4a

4-bar phrase from "Rule, Britannia".

Ex. 4b

5-bar phrase from a Scottish traditional song.

Ex. 4c

Ex. 4d

Further examples:

3-bar phrases:

Brahms — *Hungarian dance (no. 3) in F* (entirely in 3-bar phrases).
String quartet in A minor, 3rd movement, bars 1-6.
ditto 4th movement, bars 1-6.

Beethoven — *String quartet in G (op. 18 no. 2),* 2nd movt., bars 1-6.

Also many Scottish folk-tunes, e.g. *Leezie Lindsay*
Tweedside
Muckin' o' Geordie's Byre.

4-bar phrases:

Mozart — *Pianoforte sonata in A (K.331)* 1st movt. bars 1-4, 5-8.

Croft — *Hymn-tune,* 'O Worship the King' (all in 4-bar phrases.)

Folk-tune — *Greensleeves.*

Beethoven — *Symphony no. 8,* 1st movt., bars 1-4, 5-8, 9-12.

5-bar phrases:

Schubert — *Pianoforte sonata in E flat (op. 122).* Trio of 3rd movt., start.

Haydn — *String quartet (op. 54 no. 1),* start of 3rd movt.

Brahms — *Variations on a theme of Haydn,* bars 1-5, 6-10 of theme.
ditto, bars 1-5 and 6-10 of each variation.
Ballade in G minor (op. 118 no. 3), bars 1-5, 6-10.

Beethoven — *Pianoforte sonata (op. 10 no. 3),* slow movt., bars 1-5.

6-bar phrases:

Hymn-tune — 'Praise to the Lord, the Almighty, the King of Creation', bars 1-6.

Liszt — *Liebestraum (no. 3 in A flat),* bars 1-6.

Mozart — *Rondo in F for pianoforte (K. 494),* bars 1-6.[5]

Wagner — Prelude to *Die Meistersinger,* bars 1-6.
'Prize Song' from *Die Meistersinger,* bars 1-6.

[5] Printed usually as finale to the incomplete piano sonata *(K.533.)*

7-bar phrases:

Haydn *Pianoforte sonata in A* (Martienssen's Edition no 29), finale, bars 1-7, 8-14, 29-35.

Wagner 'Prize Song' from *Die Meistersinger*, bars 7-13.

Extension of phrases

Consider the following grammatical clauses:

(a) . . . . he is a big man . . . .
(b) . . . . he is a big, handsome man . . . .
(c) . . . . he is a big, handsome, muscular, sunburnt man . . . .
(d) . . . . he is a big man with a long beard . . . .
(e) . . . . he is a big man with a long, long beard . . . .

In (a) we have a statement of the plain straightforward kind which may be compared to a plain musical phrase; (b)-(e) show certain ways in which this plain phrase can be amplified or extended. (b) expands the middle of the phrase by the addition of an adjective; (c) continues the same process to greater lengths; (d) adopts a different expedient, and qualifies or amplifies the noun; while (e) expands this amplification (d) itself.

This process of expansion of a clause bears sufficient resemblance to a common musical practice to be useful as an illustration, but no more. Composers have brought variety of rhythm into their work by taking phrases and stretching them out over a larger number of bars by various methods of expansion, the most frequently found of which correspond roughly to the four literary examples given above.

Ex. 5a

Ex. 5b

Ex. 5c

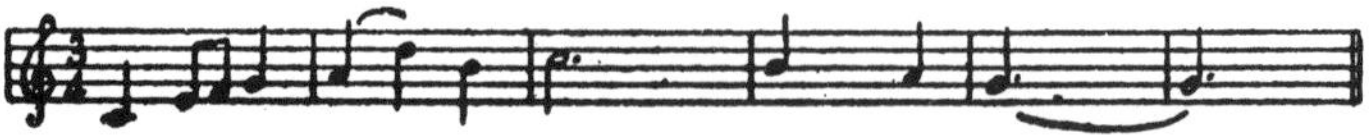

Ex. 5d

Ex. 5e

The lettering of the above examples corresponds to that of the five clauses. The plain phrase (a) is amplified at (b) by the sequential repetition of a bar; at (c) by the extension of this one extra bar to four; at (d) by a stretching of the cadence, and at (e) by a repetition of this stretched cadence. Examples of these methods are to be found frequently in classical music, as well as one or two more unusual methods of expansion; the examples given should be enough to guide the student in his examination of the following list of expanded phrases, *which must be played, not just looked at.*

Cases parallel to example 5(b)

Haydn *String quartet (op. 3 no. 5),* 3rd movt., bars 5-10.
ditto, *(op. 54 no. 1),* 4th movt., bars 45-50 and 78-82.

Cases parallel to example 5(c)

Nursery Song 'Where are you going to, my pretty maid,' bars 5-10.
Schubert *Octet,* 1st movt., bars 65-71.
Beethoven *Pianoforte sonata (op. 2 no. 2),* 2nd movt., bars 13-19.
Pianoforte sonata (op. 7), 2nd movt., bars 15-20.[6]
Pianoforte sonata (op. 10 no. 3), 3rd movt., bars 33-43.
Pianoforte sonata (op. 26), 3rd movt., bars 25-30.

[6] This example happens to show at bar 20 a further extension, carried out by interrupting the cadence, interpolating extra matter, and returning to the cadence, this time to complete it.

Cases parallel to example 5(d)

Brahms	*Symphony no. 1,* 3rd movt., bars 1-5 and 6-10.
Beethoven	*Symphony no. 4,* 1st movt., bars 43-51.
	String quartet (op. 18 no. 3), 2nd movt. Compare bars 5-12 with bars 1-4.
Handel	*Messiah,* 'He was despised'. Compare 38-39 with 41-43.

Cases parallel to example 5(e)

Brahms	*String quartet in A minor,* last movt., bars 7-13. An interesting case of a 3-bar phrase expanded to 7 by repetitions of the cadence.
	Intermezzo in A minor (op. 116 no. 2), bars 5-9.
Beethoven	*Pianoforte sonata (op. 2 no. 2),* 2nd movt., bars 72-80.

The Sentence

While the phrase may be regarded as the smallest intelligible musical unit, there can seldom be more satisfaction in contemplating such a short utterance, than is provided by the recalling of a favourite line of poetry. The intellect and the emotions alike require that two or more phrases should be put together, to balance one another and to add to one another's meaning; as in literature, where logically-connected clauses are built up into intelligible sentences, so in music the first step towards the making of continuous sense consists in putting together two or more phrases to make a musical sentence. The simplest sentences consist of two balanced phrases, statement and response:

Ex. 6

Note that word 'balanced'; it is rarely that phrases whose outward characteristics are entirely different can be combined into a satisfactory sentence.[7]

Let us look at the well-known nursery song:

The north wind doth blow, and we shall have snow,
And what will the robin do then, poor thing?
He'll sit in a barn and keep himself warm,
And hide his head under his wing, poor thing.

Analysis of this stanza shows us that it divides into two exactly balanced halves; the first half a question, to which the second half is the answer or complement. The first half is *incomplete* without the second, while the second has little meaning without the first. Not only so, but the ends of the two sections are so contrived as to correspond to one another by being in rhyme, while the first clause or phrase of each half contains an internal rhyme, 'blow' with 'snow' and 'barn' with 'warm'.

Now observe that the simple tune to which these words are sung is made in exactly the same way as the verse:

Ex. 7

It is in two 4-bar halves, each a complete phrase, of which the first, ending on a note away from the tonic chord, is incomplete; while the second, ending on the tonic, is its com-

[7] Instances do occur, however, as in the opening bars of Mozart's *Piano sonata K.332,* a perfect example of a sentence of three apparently unconnected phrases. See also the Berlioz example quoted by Macpherson, *Form in Music,* p. 28.

pletion. The 'cadences' at the ends of the phrases are rhythmically akin, as in the poem, and (a detail within the phrase, but important as a point of construction), the first half of each phrase is made up of two little fragments of melody linked together in a way which quite clearly reflects the rhyme within the first and third lines.

The above example illustrates, in the smallest possible way, one of the two basic propositions of musical design; that is to say, it consists of the statement of something in itself incomplete, balanced by a further answering statement which finishes the sense.

In music the sense of completeness (or otherwise) depends, technically speaking, upon the nature of the cadence at the end of the passage; the first phrase above ends in a way which implies dominant harmony, that is, with an imperfect cadence; the answering phrase quite clearly calls for a tonic finish—whether plagal or perfect is of no consequence, since either gives that feeling of rest in the home key which conveys the impression of completed sense.

The feeling of incompleteness at the cadence, which is the main driving force of music, and which is the composer's means of avoiding the mental sensation that his music is chopped up into small pieces, can be achieved either by an inconclusive cadence in the tonic key, or by modulating to a new key. In the latter case a cadence which, taken in isolation, might have a final effect, will not sound so in its context. For the close juxtaposition of the new key to the old will still leave the listener with the feeling that he is 'away from home' and he will feel the same psychological urge to hear the continuation as if the cadence had been an imperfect one in the home-key. In the case of a modulating first phrase, the answering phrase will return quickly to the home-key and continue there. It is impossible to over-emphasise the importance of these fundamental facts for the understanding of music, and it is necessary that students should play and sing many simple tunes to themselves, and listen to others doing so, concentrating on these contrasted effects of unrest and repose at the phrase-endings. The following examples will show the way; they will not in themselves provide nearly sufficient practice.

Sentences with non-modulating opening phrases:

Milgrove *'Harts'*, the hymn tune sometimes sung to 'Let us with a gladsome mind'.
Brahms *Variations on a theme of Haydn*, bars 1-10 of the theme and of each variation.
Mozart *Pianoforte sonata in A (K.331)*, 1st movt., bars 1-8.
Chopin *Nocturne in B (op. 32 no. 1)*, bars 1-8.
Beethoven *Pianoforte sonata (op. 2 no. 1)*, 2nd movt., bars 1-8.

Sentences with modulating opening phrases:

Wm.Horsley *Hymn-tune*, 'There is a green hill far away'.
Purcell *Rejoice in the Lord alway* (1st 12 bars from entry of the voices).
Beethoven *Pianoforte sonata (op. 2 no. 2)*, 3rd movt., bars 1-8.
Pianoforte sonata (op. 10 no. 3), 2nd movt., bars 1-9 (5 plus 4).
Schubert *Moment Musical in A flat (op. 94 no. 6)*, bars 1-16. Note that these are 8-bar phrases, owing to Schubert's having written in 3/4 time what is obviously a 6/4 melody).
Grieg *In der Heimat (Lyric Pieces, op. 43 no. 3)*.

Sentences whose opening phrases lean very strongly to the dominant key, without really modulating:

Mozart "La ci darem la mano" from *Don Giovanni*, bars 1-8.
Beethoven *Pianoforte sonata (op. 13)*, 2nd movt., bars 1-8.

While it is true that many folk-songs and other simple tunes are built on the above pattern, and that untold numbers of larger musical compositions begin with, or include, sentences so framed, there are, of course, all kinds of more complex types of sentence, as there are all kinds of methods of constructing stanzas of verse, or sentences of prose. The only effective method by which the student can come to understand these details of construction and design, is by experiencing them for himself, and the following lists, roughly classified, must be supplemented by examination of, and careful listening to, all kinds of music that come his way.

Sentences composed of three phrases:

Ex. 8

Note should be taken of the balance of the three phrases in the above example; the first and second are in exact rhythmic correspondence, while the third, after breaking new rhythmic ground, reverts for its cadence to the rhythmic pattern laid down at the start. Other schemes will be seen in the following:

Arne	*Rule Britannia,* verse.
Beethoven	*Symphony no. 8,* 1st movt., bars 1-12.
	Pianoforte sonata (op. 78), 2nd movt., bars 1-12.
	Pianoforte sonata (op. 10 no. 1), 3rd movt., bars 17-28
	Pianoforte sonata (op. 10 no. 2), 1st movt., bars 1-12
Chopin	*Mazurka in B flat (op. 7, no. 1),* bars 1-12.

Sentences composed of four phrases:

Schumann	*Arabesque (op. 18),* bars 1-16.
Beethoven	*Pianoforte sonata (op. 79),* 2nd movt., bars 1-8 (four 2-bar phrases)
Chopin	*Mazurka in F sharp minor (op. 6 no. 1),* bars 1-16.
	Waltz in C sharp minor (op. 64 no. 2) bars 1-16.
	ditto, bars 49-64.

So far, for ease of comprehension and illustration, the examples given have been sentences built of phrases of equal length, and mostly of the common four-bar type. It is, however, by no means unusual for composers to write sentences of two or more phrases of unequal length, and indeed some composers, notably Purcell, Haydn and Schubert, seem to have taken particular delight in the rhythmic freedom which a master can impart to his work by devising such 'irregular' sentences. The following are interesting examples, and the student should be on the alert to spot others:

(Unless otherwise stated, read from the start of the movement; the figures in brackets represent the number of bars in each phrase.)

Nursery song	*A frog he would a-wooing go* (4, 6. A common type)
Purcell	*I attempt from love's sickness to fly* (5, 3, 4)
Haydn	*String quartet (op. 76 no. 3),* 3rd movt., (5, 7).
Mozart	*Symphony no. 40,* 3rd movt., (3, 3, 4, 4).
Beethoven	*Pianoforte sonata (op. 2 no. 1),* 3rd movt., bars 1-14 (4, 4, 6).
	ditto, bars 41-50 (4, 6).
	Pianoforte sonata (op. 22), 2nd movt., bars 13-18 (2, 4)
	Pianoforte sonata (op. 10 no. 3), 2nd movt., (5, 4)
Schubert	*Gretchen am Spinnrade* (4, 5).
	Hark, hark, the lark (4, 6).
	Pianoforte trio in B flat, 1st movt., (5, 7).
	ditto 2nd movt., bars 3-13 (4, 4, 3).
	Morgengruss (6, 4, 6).
Brahms	*Intermezzo in C (op. 119 no. 3)* (3, 4, 5).
	String quartet in A minor, last movt., (3, 3, 7).

Moreover, somewhat exceptional cases occur in which more than four phrases of regular or irregular length are grouped into single long sentences. Notable instances are the Sailor's Song which opens Act III of Purcell's *Dido and Aeneas* (5, 3, 4, 4, 4, 4, 5), the trio of the 3rd movement of Schubert's *Octet* (5 phrases of 4 bars each) and the second part of the 'Prize Song' from Wagner's *Die Meistersinger,* which, (like many of Wagner's long stretches of melody), is difficult to analyse with certainty, but may probably best be described as 4, 4, 5, 4, 5, 6, 4 bars. In these and all other irregular groupings it is immaterial whether some or all of the phrases are extensions of shorter originals.

Finally there is the device known as 'overlapping', whereby one phrase or sentence closes into the next, its last chord being also the first chord of its successor. This technical means of achieving continuity is far more commonplace than most text-books would lead us to believe; the works of Beethoven, for instance, are littered with examples. On the other hand, it has often been used in a manner which impels us to take delight in the device *as a device.* Some illustrations follow:

Schubert	*Pianoforte trio in B flat,* 1st movt., bars 59-77. At bar 68, this 10-bar sentence ends, and its repetition begins, giving us the mathematical curiosity of two 10-bar sentences occupying only 19 bars.
Sibelius	*En Saga,* at bar 211. Similar to the Schubert example.
Mozart	*String quartet K. 575,* last movt., bars 1-19. Here an 8-bar strain is repeated, and at its final cadence closes into a repetition of its own last 4 bars. Thus 8 plus 8 overlapping 4 add up to a total of 19.
Beethoven	*Symphony no. 6,* last movement at bar 32. *Pianoforte sonata (op. 14 no. 2),* 1st movt. at bar 33.

II

THE TWO BASIC FORMS

WHEN WE SPEAK of 'basic forms', there is an implication that all music since their establishment shows some traceable connection with one or other of these forms. This implication we may accept, subject to two qualifications. The first is, that from the time of Liszt and Berlioz, in the middle of the nineteenth century, conscious and deliberate attempts have been made to avoid such connections; these attempts have continued to the present day, with varying degrees of success. The second is, that many pieces of music written to words (though far from all such pieces), rely upon the literary structure to provide a satisfactory form for the work of art as a whole, and pay little heed to niceties of musical design *as such.* The artist relying on this means of achieving unity is undertaking a grave responsibility, for he runs the risk of not only failing to achieve a satisfactory musical design, but of ruining the effect of a beautifully wrought piece of verse. Such compositions range from short songs to whole operas.

During the past half-century it has been customary to classify the majority of short pieces as either 'binary' or 'ternary', according as they are divisible into two, or into three, fairly clearly defined sections. A 'binary' form is said to consist of two roughly equal parts, the second an 'answer' to the first in much the same way as the second phrase of a sentence may 'answer' the first. Very sketchy and vague generalisations are perforce accepted as to the connection between the two parts, as that 'the second part would be based on material similar to the first'; or, more specifically, that it would 'carry on and bring to a conclusion the musical idea announced by the first'.[8] By contrast, a 'ternary' form is said

[8] Macpherson, *Form in Music,* p. 62.

to consist of the statement of an idea, followed by a second, contrasted idea, and the whole rounded off by a re-statement of the original idea; a kind of musical sandwich. It is pointed out, almost as if it ought to be taken for granted, that the second is obviously a more satisfactory and more highly organised structure. Folk-tunes, hymn tunes, simple dances and the like, are freely called upon for illustration of the 'binary' form, while such short pieces as items from Schumann's *Album for the Young* and the simpler *Songs without Words* of Mendelssohn usually furnish adequate examples of 'ternary' form.

This classification, so far as the writer is aware, was first expounded by Hadow in his *Sonata Form,* and was based upon apparent inconsistencies in the older or traditional use of the expressions 'binary' and 'ternary', inconsistencies whose existence it would be idle to deny.[9] The author begs respectfully to differ with Hadow on the matter of principle, and to suggest that by retaining the expressions 'binary' and 'ternary' with modified meaning, he sowed the seeds of a confusion which Tovey's emphatic re-assertion of the older meaning of the terms has only made worse.[10]

As will be seen from what follows, the author firmly believes that the older method of *classification* is more in line with the facts of our music, but suggests that it is necessary to make a clean sweep of the bad terminology which is the despair of students who take the trouble to read more than one authority, and find the same words meaning entirely different things, according to the particular writer's standpoint.

Hadow's classification seems on the face of it to meet the facts of tiny musical situations such as those mentioned above, and will in fact do fairly well for work on a small scale. But when careful attention is given to the real mental effect of such pieces when closely *listened to,* rather than examined in print, it is revealed as superficial. For one thing, it begs the question of the relationship between the two parts

[9] Hadow, *Sonata Form,* preface.
[10] Tovey, *Musical Articles from the* Enc. Brit. pp 208-209.

of the 'binary' form. For another, it is altogether too 'water-tight', and leaves too much unexplained when we meet more complicated musical organisations which spring from the same roots; i.e. one's consideration of more highly-organised designs has to begin again from scratch, without any firm foundations in the facts of the history of the development of musical structure. Such a course is bound to lead to trouble, and has done; has, in fact, been an obstacle to the fullest enjoyment of music for countless people whose understanding of 'musical form' has been built up on the appearance rather than the sound of the music. Theorists have overlooked the fact once again, that music is something which occupies time, not space; that the printed copy is not the music, but merely the system of continuous signals to the performer as to what he is to do next.

Consider the following four cases: (Example 9).

Hadow's classification would call (a) and (b) 'ternary', (c) 'binary', and for (d) would be forced to some cross-bred expression like 'binary shape existing together with ternary idea',[11] by virtue of there being two balanced parts, the second of which is partly made up of a return to the first idea. The implication is that (a) and (b) are identical in shape, and that they and (d) are more 'satisfactory' or more 'symmetrical' than (c); as if musical symmetry, like the symmetry of a wash-hand basin, were something that could be gauged by means of a measuring tape.

Now let us consider the matter afresh. Listen carefully to the first parts of (a) and (d) with an unprejudiced mind, and you will find that they leave you without any particular expectation of anything more to follow—the sentences are complete in themselves, and it is a matter of indifference whether they are followed up or not. The most one could do would be to play something else by way of a change; in which case, one would *have* to return to the first idea to give any real point to the digression; which is exactly what does happen in both cases.

[11] Macpherson, *Form in Music*, p. 87.

Ex. 9a

Ex. 9b

Ex. 9c

" *Kelvingrove*"

Ex. 9d

Turn now to (b) and (c). Their case is quite different, for if you listen attentively to *their* first sentences, but do not continue any further, you will be left with a most definite impression that there ought to be more to come; and you will have a feeling of frustration if you do not get it.

Observe that, whereas the first sentences of (a) and (d) came to a full stop at home on the tonic chord, these two do not; (b) ends its first part most distinctly in another key from that in which it started, while (c) though possibly still centred on its home-tonic (though this is doubtful) has certainly paused somewhere else than on that tonic. There is here no sense of completeness, and if artistic violence is not to be done, there is an imperative *need* for a continuation. In (b) this happens to take the form of a digression and return to the original first strain; in (c), we have a return to the stability of tonic harmonies by a slightly devious route. To sum up, we find that in (a), a 'ternary' form *and in (d),* a 'binary' form (even though incorporating the 'ternary' idea), the continuation was not necessary, however pleasant, while in (b), a 'ternary' form *and in (c)* a 'binary' one, a continuation of some sort was actually required to complete the musical sense.

The essential point is not whether the original first tune returns again in whole or in part at the end of the piece, but whether the first part of the piece ends at home or away from home.

So far as the author is aware, attention was first strongly drawn and directed to the distinction between pieces having a first-part ending 'at home' and those having a first-part ending 'away from home' by Tovey; though other writers, notably Sir Hubert Parry, were writing soundly on the subject in works less widely read than those of Tovey.[12]

It is proposed here to discard the expressions 'binary' and 'ternary', and to refer to the type whose first part ends at home as 'closed' and that whose first part ends away from home as 'open'. We are then free to add the words '2-part' or '3-part' according as there is a re-statement of the first part at the end or not. Of our four examples on pages 33-34, (a) and (d) are therefore simple 'closed 3-part forms'; (b) is a simple 'open 3-part form' and (c) an 'open 2-part' form. The 'closed 2-part form' exists only in tunes of the most primitive kind, such as 'Baa, baa, black sheep'.

Here we have a classification which cuts across that which has been accepted since Hadow's book appeared, and yet retains that part of it which arose from genuinely unsatisfactory features of the traditional one. Such a classification seems far better, because it not only accords with the superficial facts of small pieces quite as well as Hadow's, but also has an important bearing on the structure of the more highly-organised musical forms which developed after these basic principles had been established. The developed lyrical forms (as we may call them) are based upon the 'closed' principle of complete statement—digression—restatement as illustrated in examples 9(a) and 9(d) above. They will be discussed in the next chapter. The *dramatic* forms, in which are cast the greatest movements of Haydn, Mozart, Beethoven and Brahms, are, on the other hand, developments of the 'open' principle, as illustrated in examples 9(b) and 9(c), where the basic idea is of an incomplete opening statement, followed by a return home by a route which can be mildly or wildly adventurous. Here the initial statement is like the first act of a play, which is concerned with laying a 'situation' before the

[12] See Parry, *Style in Musical Art,* chapter xv.

audience; the adventures and safe return of the second part correspond to the working-out of the dramatic possibilities of the 'situation' in the second act of the play, and the *dénouement* or resolution in the third.

Until the student has grasped the distinction between these two basic methods of building up a musical composition, there is really very little point in his proceeding any further, since a clear realisation of this distinction (based upon experience, not upon theory), is absolutely vital for all subsequent understanding of musical design. He is advised to spend considerable time and trouble playing and *listening to* the pieces of music in the list at the end of this chapter, and in observing especially the psychological effect of the endings of the first parts. His time will not be wasted, and his reward will be great.

One or two details had better be mentioned for the student's guidance in making his analyses. First, it is usually, but not invariably the case that the sections of these little pieces are repeated, i.e. played twice through; the idea doubtless has its origins in the need for making the pieces sufficiently long to command serious attention. In the two-part form, the matter is straightforward enough—each section is repeated as soon as it has been played, thus—|: a :||: b :|. In the three-part forms, whether 'open' or 'closed', the first section is played and repeated, then the middle and final sections are played once through, and then both repeated, thus—|: a :||: ba :|. This is easily enough followed where formal repeat-marks are employed in the printing; often, however, the repeats are written-out in full, and in many cases embellishments or minor alterations of one kind or another are introduced into the repeat. The student must bear this in mind when *reading* the copy; when listening to the music there is rarely any difficulty in recognising a repeat at once. Cases also occur in which the first section, after coming to a half-close, is repeated, but with a full-close. Since the end of the repeat is the real end of the first section, these cases come within the 'closed' category. [See, for example, the first

16 bars of Beethoven's *Pianoforte Sonata in A flat (op. 26).*]

Second, the baldness of outline of the strict forms is sometimes modified a little by the addition of an 'introduction' or a 'coda' or both. In little pieces such as those under consideration, these are rarely likely to be more than a bar or two of introductory or closing chords; but they must be accounted for in a formal analysis of the piece, and not allowed to confuse the main issue. For an example of such a coda, see no. 17 in Schumann's *Album for the Young*; and for both introduction and coda, see no. 36 of the same work. Mendelssohn, in his *Songs without Words*, nos. 4 and 9, uses the same phrase for both introduction *and* coda; these two pieces, incidentally, being almost identical as to the details of their shape.

Examples of the simple 'closed' forms:

(N.B. In the examples by Beethoven, the minuet[13] *or* the trio, taken as a separate movement, is to be understood; not the whole movement.)

Schumann	*Album for the Young*, nos. 3, 5, 6, 8, 9, 16, 20, 24, 26.
Grieg	*Poetic tone-pictures (op. 3)*, nos. 1, 3, 5.
	Lyric pieces (op. 12), no. 7.
Beethoven	*Pianoforte sonata (op. 2 no 2)*, the scherzo.
	Pianoforte sonata (op. 10 no. 3), the minuet.
	Pianoforte sonata (op. 22), the minuet.
	Pianoforte sonata (op. 26), the scherzo.
	Pianoforte sonata (op. 26), 1st movt., the theme and each variation taken separately. (N.B. In this case only the first part is repeated.)
Chopin	*Nocturne in E flat (op. 9 no. 2)*. (NB. bars 25-34 are coda.)

Examples of the simple 'open' forms:

Schumann	*Album for the Young*, nos. 1, 2, 7, 11, 15, 17, 19, 21, 22, 25, 28, 38.
Grieg	*Poetic tone-pictures, (op. 3)*, no. 2.
	Lyric Pieces (op. 12), nos. 2 and 4, and *(op. 43)* nos. 1, 4, 5.

[13] The term 'minuet' is to be taken here as including 'scherzo'.

Beethoven *Pianoforte sonata (op. 2 no. 1),* the minuet.
ditto. the trio.
Pianoforte sonata (op. 2 no. 2), the trio only.
Pianoforte sonata (op. 2 no. 3), the scherzo.
ditto. the trio.
Pianoforte sonata (op. 14 no. 2), 2nd movt., theme and each variation.
Pianoforte sonata (op. 26), the trio.
Pianoforte sonata (op. 28), the scherzo.
ditto. the trio.
Pianoforte sonata (op. 31 no. 3), the menuetto.
ditto. the trio.

III

EXPANSION OF THE 'CLOSED' PRINCIPLE

THE BASIC IDEA of the simple 'closed' 3-part form (we may ignore the 'closed' 2-part form), that of complete statement, digression and re-statement, underlies several more extended types of musical structure which have fulfilled important functions at one period or another in the history of our music.

This chapter will deal with four such types, each of which has anatomical features common to large numbers of movements of the most diverse kinds. These four are usually known as:

1. The aria form or *da capo* form.
2. The minuet-and-trio form.
3. The episodical form.
4. The simple rondo form.

All of them display the same initial feature; that is, a first main section complete in itself, and capable of being detached without leaving in the hearer a sense of frustration. This section may be long or short, and may itself be built up on a more or less elaborate plan, but in no case will it call imperatively for a continuation. Hence all such forms, in the last resort, are to a great or small extent 'sectional' in feeling, and although much subtlety of craftsmanship and technical skill may be used in disguising or minimising this feeling, it can scarcely be entirely abolished.

It follows that *complete* organic unity cannot be attained within a movement so constructed, and these forms are therefore one and all most suitable for the conveying of lyrical rather than dramatic musical ideas. Indeed, they are sometimes known as 'lyric forms', and upon them are based countless thousands of short pieces, dances, solo vocal movements, and the lesser movements of big-scale works such as sonatas, string quartets and symphonies. This is not to say that much great music has not been written upon such lines; indeed, most of Bach's and Handel's most moving arias are in the *da capo* form; many of Chopin's works, of Brahms's subtle piano pieces, and of the loveliest classical slow movements are in 'episodical form', while a small handful of extremely powerful pieces, besides myriads of smaller things, owe a great part of their very power to the stark, straightforward lines of the 'simple rondo'. In such cases it will be seen that the 'simplicity' is not incompatible with great and sometimes violent emotional feeling; such emotions being, however, always of a straightforward kind.

These forms, then, have their limitations, and it is from the 'open' basis, with the driving force that lies in its incomplete opening section, that (as we shall see) the subtlest things in music are derived.[14]

Let us examine the four forms one at a time.

1. *The aria form, or* da capo *form.*

The names come from the fact that so many of the arias in the operas of Alessandro Scarlatti and Handel, and in the church music of the latter and of Bach (to say nothing of multitudes of lesser composers) are conventionally in this form, and that so stereotyped was the method of 'restatement' that composers usually did not trouble to write beyond the end of the 'digression', merely indicating by the words 'da capo' ('from the beginning') that the first section should be performed again. As a matter of fact, the main section of the 'da capo' aria is often of itself a very subtle thing indeed, with a special type of internal organisation of its own, and will be considered in a later chapter. Taken *as a whole,*

[14] This is *not* confusing the issue, as Macpherson would have us believe. (*Form in Music,* p. 92, f.n.) On the contrary, as the student who has given time and attention to the previous chapter will easily see, it is to put the theory of the matter into line with the actual experience of attentive listening, as against the superficialities of appearance in print, or of half-concentrated attention.

however, it is the crudest of all the 'closed' forms, no attempt whatever being made to reduce the tedium of the complete re-statement, which often has the air of being a perfunctory formality.[15] The boredom which we nowadays suffer on the rare occasions when such an aria is given in full is a proof which theorists seem to have overlooked, that the 'sandwich' form is not necessarily well-balanced or satisfactory at all; far from it. The modern custom of drastically curtailing the *da capo* by playing only the instrumental introduction (which, invariably coming to a full close in the tonic, makes a thoroughly satisfying end) provides not only the necessary balance of key, but also sufficient of a recollection of the original subject-matter, and is thus a positive contribution to shapeliness, in contrast to the full *da capo* which is liable to be no more than a sprawling convention.

Here is further proof of our need to bear always in mind that music exists in time, not space, and that it cannot be judged outside of time; one can *see* at a glance that a pyramid is symmetrical, and an attempt to form a mental picture of a complete *da capo* aria in a single moment's thought may give just as perfect a feeling of symmetry as the pyramid; but that feeling will be entirely belied by the actual experience of the ear, when it is called upon to listen to the unabridged thing itself, except in cases (such as Handel's 'Where'er you walk') where the whole piece is fairly short. For the ear, being satisfied by the return to the main key of the piece, and by a sufficient reminder of the *matter* of the main section, will lose interest in the mechanical re-statement of everything that originally followed, and in particular will resent being once again taken through the same system of modulations. The reaction of boredom will be none the less real for its cause being unrecognised or felt only subconsciously. Let the student prove this by experiment with any *da capo* aria (e.g. the

[15] Handel in his later oratorios often indicates 'D.S.' *(dal segno)* instead of *da capo*, thereby partly reducing the restatement by omitting its opening. But in an early oratorio like *Esther*, 9 out of its 11 arias have the full *da capo*, while in the opera *Giulio Cesare* (chosen at random), all but two of the 33 arias have the conventional D.C.

wonderful Cradle Song from part 2 of Bach's *Christmas Oratorio, or* 'He was despised' from Handel's *Messiah*); and having so satisfied himself, let him rest content not to enquire into the interior structure of the individual sections until he reaches Chapter 6.

2. *The minuet-and-trio form.*

Here, the simple 'closed' 3-part form is expanded by multiplication. We have in the minuet a *complete statement*; in the trio which follows it, a digression or *contrasted statement;* and a re-statement consisting of a return of the first section in full, this return being usually indicated, as in the aria form, by a verbal formula such as 'Menuetto da capo'; a concession to our sense of the shortness of life being usually made in the omission of the repeats which were played in the opening section. *Each of these three sections is in itself a complete form* of one or other kind on a small scale. To put it diagramatically:

A	B	A2
(Minuet)	(Trio)	(Minuet)
|:a:||:ba:| *or* |:a:||:b:|	|:c:||:dc:| *or* |:c:||:d:|	aba *or* ab

Nothing could be more straightforward, more easily comprehended in theory, or more easily followed by the ear in practice; within each main section there is scope for just as much subtlety as can be found in the simple forms, and no more: phrase-lengths may be diverse, modulations may be effective and interesting, and the return of the sub-sections which are designated 'a' and 'c' may be varied, decorated or extended. None the less, the fact remains that the form tends from its very nature to be four-square, and it is therefore rarely found except in the minuet (or scherzo) movements of sonatas and symphonies, or in short pieces of a rather formal kind.[16] Occasionally, it is true, the composer's intention in movements other than these may be most satisfactorily carried out in just such a rigid manner; such a case is the

[16] As, for example, the 6th of Schubert's *Moments Musicaux, (op. 94)*, his *Impromptu in A flat, (op. 142 no. 2)*, or Chopin's *Polonaise in A major*.

Funeral March which forms the slow movement of Beethoven's *Pianoforte sonata in A flat (op. 26),* a movement which from its title and nature would seem to call for considerable squareness of treatment.[17]

No very useful purpose can at this stage be served by studying very many of such movements from the score; the student should, however, at once and at all available future opportunities, make a point of listening to them at concerts, by radio or gramophone, taking care to follow mentally all the sections, including the repeats, so that he can tell where he is at any moment; and carefully listening for the effects of key-contrasts, both within and between main sections.

Caution. Though the vast majority of classical minuet and scherzo-movements conform to type, there are exceptions, such as the following:

Beethoven	*Pianoforte sonata (op. 31 no. 3),* where the scherzo is in sonata form.	
Beethoven	*Symphonies nos. 4 and 7,* where the trio is twice alternated with the scherzo thus: A-B-A2-B2-A3.	
Mozart	*Clarinet Quintet.*	In all these, there are *two* trios alternating with the main section, thus: A-B-A2-C-A3.
Schumann	*Symphonies nos. 1 and 2.*	
Brahms	*Scherzo, (op. 4) for piano.*	

3. *The Episodical Form.*

This, to put it crudely, is the minuet-and-trio form with the corners rounded off. The EPISODE corresponds to the trio, in that it is a middle-section, independent of the main or first part of the piece, both as to key and matter; sometimes also differing from it in pace and metre.[18]

The minuet-and-trio form is by its very simplicity of outline a most satisfactory vehicle for the expression of

[17] Beethoven's other and greater Funeral March, in his *3rd Symphony,* though on a vastly greater scale, is likewise cast in a form which is clean-cut in its effect—the simple rondo form.

[18] 'Episode' is one of those unfortunate words which have several different meanings in music, according to the context. We shall meet it again in other contexts, with other meanings. It shares this disability with 'tone', 'inversion' and 'codetta', to mention the more outstanding cases.

simple lyrical ideas at not-too-great length; on the other hand, it is somewhat rigid, it emphasises the sectional nature of its structure, and it therefore tends to interfere with rather than encourage a sense of continuity. Hence, composers have adopted every kind of device of technique to overcome these characteristics in cases where they would show up as defects; to smooth over the joins, to make the various sections flow into one another, or to prepare the way for each other; to eliminate unnecessary repeats, to write *codas* for the purpose of rounding off the whole, or *introductions* to create the proper mood before the main business begins; and so on.

Many cases lie on the border-line between minuet-and-trio form and episodical form, being more-or-less clear-cut in outline, yet having connecting passages (or 'links') between sections, and other details designed to give a certain sense of continuity. Let us look closely at two such border-line cases:

(a) Chopin, Nocturne in G minor, op. 37 no. 1.

The main section extends from bar 1 to bar 40, being a simple 'closed' 3-part form ('a', 1-8, 'b' 9-16, 'a2' 17-24; repeat of 'b,a2', 25-40.) The middle section is ushered in by a move from the tonic of the main section to the dominant or threshold of the new key (bar 40, last beat), which of itself has the effect of *preparing the way* for the new section. The middle part (i.e., the 'trio' or 'episode' is centred in the related key of E flat, and like the main section, is itself a simple 'closed' 3-part form ('c' 41-48, 'd' 49-56, 'c2' 57-64.) But observe that the last strain of 'c2' is modified in two ways: first of all, the movement is halted three times by pauses, the effect of which is to indicate that something important is about to happen; and second, the harmony of the last two bars is altered and darkened (the melody remaining as before), so as to achieve a smoother junction of the returning minor. In fact, it leads to the dominant of the original key, upon which a 2-bar linking section poises itself, heightening the effect of suspense and of satisfaction at the ultimate restoration of the old G minor tonality, and the original first melody. Thus the final section (A2) arrives (bars 67-90), being but for very minor changes of decorative detail, an exact copy of A, but without the repeat of 'ba2'. The piece is rounded off by a minute coda consisting of one bar's additional cadence and a *tierce de Picardie*.

(b) Chopin, Fantaisie-Impromptu in C sharp minor, op. 66.

In this case, though the structure is almost as clearly-defined as is the case with the Nocturne, the nature of the material, the care taken to smooth over the joins, and the more elaborate introduction and coda, leave one in no doubt as to its being episodical rather than minuet-and-trio form.

The following method of formal descriptive analysis, which will be employed in future in this book, is one which the student will be well advised to adopt in his own work; it has the merits of clarity and succinctness.

Bars 1-4	Introduction, defining the tonic and setting the mood.
Bars 5-41 'A'	Main section, an 'open' 3-part form divided as follows: 'a' 5-12, first part closing in dominant 'b' 13-24, second part, moving through E major back to the tonic 'a2' 25-41, restatement of first part, which after 5 bars develops and extends by sequence to a highly dramatic dash down the keyboard into a full close in the tonic major, closing into:
Bars 41-42	Introduction to the middle section, the first bar being also the last of the main section. (An 'overlap')
Bars 43-82 'B'	Episode or middle section in the tonic major key, and in a very straightforward closed 3-part form: 'c' 43-50 first part, repeated 51-58 'd' 59-62 second part 'c2' 63-70 restatement of 'c' 71-82 repeat of 'd,c2' The expected full close does not arrive at bar 82, which instead remains on the dominant, which is also the dominant of the original key. Hence the next move is completely prepared for, the middle section being not separated from it, but leading to it.
Bars 83-119 'A2'	Restatement of first section, exact in every detail
Bars 119-138 CODA	Coda, overlapped by 'A2' exactly as 'B' was overlapped by 'A'. Observe the construction of the coda, which keeps up the semiquaver figuration of the main section throughout, gradually subsiding in mood

Bars 119-138 CODA *contd.*	{	until, at bar 129, *the melody of the middle section* is introduced in the bass. Thus the two sections are united in the last few bars, a fact which gives to the coda a relevance and artistic purpose which fully justifies its considerable length.

The student may now with profit analyse and study the following straightforward examples of episodical form, none of which is very far removed from the minuet-and-trio:

Beethoven	*Pianoforte sonata (op. 28)*, slow movement. (One of Beethoven's comparatively few examples).
Chopin	*Impromptu in A flat (op. 29).*
	Nocturne in C minor (op. 48 no. 1).
Schubert	*Moment Musical in C major (op. 94 no. 1).*
Brahms	*Intermezzo in A major (op. 76 no. 6).*

The episodical form, however, is capable of conveying musical ideas in a subtler and more unified way than has been shown so far, beautiful as some of the above pieces are. Brahms, more than any other composer, found that lyrical ideas could be naturally grouped and developed along such lines, and his piano works (among which are some of the most exquisite short pieces of music ever written), as well as the lesser movements of his big works, afford numerous examples. Needless to say, although all grow upon the basic anatomical framework, no two are really alike in design. Brahms shows the most consummate skill in avoiding the feeling of sectional building, and in giving coherence to the whole piece and relevance to every individual part of it. No better examples can be found than the three *Intermezzi, (op. 117);* opinions will differ as to the relative merits of the three, but the author, finding no. 3 to be, for him, the pinnacle of Brahms's achievement in this direction, uses it here for detailed examination. The student will do well to examine the other two equally closely, in addition to the examples given at the end of this section.

Brahms—Intermezzo in C sharp minor, op. 117 no. 3.

Bars 1-45 'A'	{	Main section, in simple 'open' 2-part form.
		1-10 1st part. A sentence of two 5-bar phrases.

Bars 1-45 'A' *contd.*	'a'		The first is unharmonised, and ends in a half-close. The answering phrase is similar, but is harmonised, and closes into the dominant key.
	'b'	11-20	2nd part. A new idea conveyed in similar terms; i.e., an unharmonised 5-bar phrase in the dominant key is answered by a harmonised 5-bar phrase closing firmly in the tonic.
		21-40	Repetition of 1-20, 'a' being now richly harmonised throughout, while 'b' is substantially unaltered.
		41-45	Coda to the main section, developed from the opening phrase of 'a', with almost static harmony over a tonic pedal.
Bars 46-75 'B'			Episode, in the submediant major (A major), in simple 'open' 3-part form.
	'c'	46-55	1st part; a 10-bar sentence in two equal and balancing phrases, closing in the dominant. Repeated exactly.
	'd'	56-65	2nd part; another 10-bar sentence in two equal phrases; the tonality is vague, though with leanings towards the related keys of F sharp minor and B minor; the last bar of this sentence runs through a discord to the dominant of A major (the present home-key) over which the next part opens.
	'c2'	66-75	Recapitulation of 1st part, modified as to its last 3 bars, reaching a half-close. 'd'-'c2' repeated exactly except for final full close.
Bars 76-81 Link			A 6-bar linking passage of great subtlety, in two 3-bar balancing parts. The first seems to be a dominant preparation for a return to the home-key of C sharp minor, but veers off to pause on an alien harmony. It includes a seemingly unimportant inner-part in semiquavers which assumes great significance in the upshot. The second part is an exact transposition of the first, one tone higher and thus apparently establishing the dominant of *D sharp minor,* but as before, veering to an irresolute pause.

Bars 82-108 'A2'	The restatement of the main section begins with the first phrase harmonised in an extraordinary manner, as if the distance of the 'irresolute pause' in bar 81 were being gradually reduced by stages, till the comforts of home are reached at bar 84.[19] We can now see the significance of the semiquaver inner part which was mentioned above; it turns out to have been a foreshadowing of the opening of the main tune, introduced casually (perhaps, originally, it was accidental) at bar 77, and gradually more and more insisted upon until it actually merges into the tune itself. The *second* phrase is expanded from the original five bars to six, in a gesture (bar 91) that seems to be one of sheer delight in the beauty of the moment. 'b' follows normally from bars 93-102 (there is no repeat), and the coda-to-the-first-part, extended to 6 bars by simple prolonging of its final chord, takes on a greater significance in rounding off the whole piece.

Enough has now been said of the episodical form, and it must be left to the student to listen to as many as he can of the following list of examples, in the light of analyses made beforehand by himself.

Chopin	*Impromptu in G flat (op. 51).*
	Nocturne in F (op. 15 no. 1).
	Nocturne in F sharp (op. 15 no. 2)
	Nocturne in F minor (op. 55 no. 1), in which 'A2' merges almost at once into coda.
Schubert	*Impromptu in A flat (op. 90 no. 4)*
Brahms	Piano pieces (*Intermezzi*, etc.):
	op. 10 no. 1.
	op. 76 no. 2
	op. 116 nos. 2 and 3

[19] The whole of the section 76-84 is one of the most remarkable instances on record of the harmonic subtlety that can be achieved through what Tovey calls the 'enhanced dominant', that is, the dominant *of the dominant*. A detailed comment upon it would be both long and out-of-place.

Brahms *contd.*
op. 117 nos. 1 and 2 (in the latter, the theme of the episode is suggested by that of the main section.)
op. 118 nos. 3 and 5 (in the latter, the episode is a set of variations upon a 4-bar theme.)
op. 119 no. 2

The student should also study the 2nd and 3rd movements of Brahms's *1st* and *3rd symphonies,* as fine examples of extended episodical forms, of varying degrees of subtlety of construction.

4. *The Simple Rondo Form.*

The essence of all rondo forms is that a complete statement given out at the start is alternated (in whole or part) with several successive contrasted sections. The species of rondo at present under consideration is called 'simple' because no higher organisation is called for than can be described in the formula ABACA(DA . . . .), where the main theme occurs at least three times, and possibly four or more times.

Of the origins of the form we need say little, save that it is obvious that the alternation of verse and chorus, of solo-section and crowd-section, must have had a great appeal at an early stage in man's communal development, from the very simplicity of the underlying structural idea. We have already noticed something on these lines in the 'minuet with two trios' mentioned on page 43, where the ABA principle was simply extended to ABACA, but it is further to be observed that the very ease with which a longish piece of music can be made on such lines, led it into favour in days when the higher organisation of instrumental music was only beginning. Thus, examples of instrumental and vocal rondos abound in the music of the 17th century; many are to be found in the operas of Lully (e.g. *Thésée,* act iv. Sc. 7), while the keyboard suites of the French *clavécinistes* (Couperin, Rameau, etc.) afford innumerable instances. Excellent examples are also to be found in the works of Bach, and if the student will examine as many as he can of the following, no more need be said about the early stages of the history of the rondo as a consciously-applied principle. The main theme recurs always in the tonic key, while the episodes are in various related keys.

Couperin	*Soeur Monique*
	Les Vendageuses
	L'Enchanteresse
	La tendre Fanchon
Rameau	*La Villageoise*
Daquin	*Le Coucou*
Purcell	Rondeau from *Abdelazer*
J. S. Bach	Rondeau from *Suite no. 2* for orchestra
	Rondeau from *Partita no. 2* for keyboard (varied returns.)
	Passepied from *English Suite no. 5*
	Gavotte from *Suite in E* for unaccompanied violin

As subtler and more highly-organised forms of music emerged, the simple rondo tended to lose ground to other forms more capable of expressing more complex ideas and moods. Notably, the classical masters developed the 'sonata-rondo', a cross-bred form which will be discussed in due course. None the less, Haydn, Mozart and Beethoven wrote some very powerful and beautiful music in the older form, of which we will analyse two examples, and list some others for the student's own consideration.

(1) Slow movement of Beethoven's 'Pathétique' sonata, (op. 13).

Bars 1-16	'A1'	The main theme, a complete 8-bar sentence in A flat major closing in the tonic, and repeated with the harmonies more sonorously spread out.
Bars 17-28	'B'	First episode, in two parts: the first, 17-23, starts in the relative minor, passes through C minor to a full close in the dominant. The second part (24-28) merely reaffirms that key twice and closes into:
Bars 29-36	'A2'	First return of the main theme; an exact re-statement of 1-8 *without repeat.*
Bars 37-50	'C'	Second episode, starting in the tonic minor, but ranging widely and dramatically via
Bars 37-50 *contd.*		F flat major (written for convenience as E major) back to the home-dominant, and closing into:

Bars 51-66	'A3'	Second return of main theme, *with* repeat, being a slightly elaborated version of 1-16, the semiquaver couplets being developed into triplets.
Bars 67-73	Coda	Consisting of five variously decorated full-closes.

The above movement shows the simple rondo-form exquisitely used for a straightforward and almost wholly lyrical movement. Let us look now at a movement on a far bigger scale, in which the mood, though lacking great depth, is vigorous and fiery:

(2) Rondo from Beethoven's 'Waldstein' sonata, op. 53.

Bars 1-62	'A1'	Main theme in C major. A complete simple 'closed' 3-part form: 'a' — 1-8 'b' — 9-23 link —24-30 'a2' —31-38 Repeat of 'ba2'—39-62
Bars 63-70		Linking passage.
Bars 71-98	'B'	First episode. A very straightforward passage in the relative minor.
Bars 99-113		Linking passage based upon the main theme, and leading back to the threshold of the home-key.
Bars 114-175	'A2'	First return of main theme. A complete re-statement, including the repeat of 'ba2'.
Bars 175-312	'C'	Second episode in two quite distinct parts: (i) 175-220, tonic minor key. 8 bars closing in A flat, repeated. 8 bar answering sentence returning to C minor, repeated. This paragraph is followed by a progressive reduction in the size of the rhythmic units, by subdivision in halves; thus, a 4-bar phrase is succeeded by twice two bars, twice one bar, and final derived single octaves; each reduction being by way of repeating the latter half of the previous unit.[20]

[20] This is a notable instance of Beethoven's way of increasing impetus by gradually shortening his rhythmic units.

Bars 175-312 *contd.*		(ii) 221-312. Plunge into A flat major, followed by a long, circuitous and highly dramatic return to the home-dominant. This part is practically entirely derived from the first phrase of the main theme, and mostly from its first 3 beats. The long 'dominant preparation' starting at bar 295 arouses a great sense of expectancy, which is gratified by:
Bars 313-344	'A3'	Second re-statement of main theme, omitting the repeat (or rather, using *only* the repeat) of 'ba2'.
Bars 345-543	Coda	A section of colossal dimensions in relation to the whole, whose details are well worth the student's study. It almost all derives from 'A'.

List of some notable movements in the simple rondo form:—

Haydn	Gypsy' rondo, from the *piano trio (no. 1) in G.* A loosely-constructed sectional movement, whose main theme is a substantial 'closed' 3-part form with repeats.
Mozart	*Rondo in A minor for pianoforte (K.511).*
	Adagio of the *piano sonata in C minor (K.457).*
Beethoven	*Rondo for pianoforte (op. 51 no.1).*
	Finale of *pianoforte sonata (op. 10 no. 3).*
	Andante in F for pianoforte.
	Rondo a capriccio for piano ('Rage over a lost halfpenny').
	Funeral March from the *3rd symphony.*

IV

EXPANSION OF THE 'OPEN' PRINCIPLE

THE HISTORY OF the slow evolution of the 'sonata form',[21] the highest type of musical organisation achieved by the classical masters, is one of the utmost complexity, which it would be out of place to examine in detail in a textbook. Nevertheless, ignorance and misunderstanding of the subject are so widespread, especially regarding the absolutely fundamental question of *tonality,* or the relationship of the various keys within the structure, that a short summary of the transition from simple 'open' forms to compound ones is necessary. This chapter, therefore, is to be regarded in the main as a preparation for the next.

(1) Development of the 'open 2-part form'.

We need not here trace the stages through which the rudimentary 2-part form discussed in chapter III passed, before it reached its highest point of development in J. S. Bach's instrumental works; it is sufficient to say that plenty of examples can be found in 16th-century instrumental music, and that the whole progress of instrumental music in the 17th century is entirely bound up with it. By the time Bach and his contemporaries were writing their innumerable " suites " of dances (almost every item of which is in the

[21] The expression 'sonata form' has come, unfortunately perhaps, to be used as meaning the underlying basic structure of the principle movements of the sonata (or string quartet, symphony, etc.). It is even sometimes referred to as 'first-movement form'. Thus, in the classical sonata, the first movement almost always, the finale very often, and the slow movement sometimes, are in 'sonata form'. Even to this rule there are exceptions: three or four of the first movements of Beethoven's piano sonatas are not in 'sonata form', while his works contain at least two scherzo-movements which are in sonata form.

" open " 2-part form), it had assumed a fairly standard pattern, easily traceable to the primitive original, somewhat as follows:

First Part	*Second Part*
An opening clause or section starting in the tonic and modulating to a related key; leading to a fairly substantial closing section quite definitely in that key.	The same opening section as the first part, now in a related key, finding its way back (perhaps through a series of modulations) to the tonic; this second part usually ends with the same closing bars as wound up the first part, but now in the tonic key.

Each part is played twice.

Examples are endless; well-known ones are the allemande and courante of Bach's *French Suite in G major*. The student is also recommended to look at the corrente of his *Partita in D major*, and at the gigues of the *Partita in B flat* and *English Suite in A minor*, as showing considerable sections in the dominant key at the end of the first part, which return at the end of the second part, but in the tonic.

Many of the preludes of Bach's '48', especially in the second book, are highly-developed instances of a similar kind.

From this it is no great step to the following, which represents the highest stage of organisation which the simple 'open' 2-part form was ever to attain; it is common among the more elaborate instrumental works of all the early eighteenth-century composers, and is the formal basis of hundreds of Domenico Scarlatti's single-movement harpsichord sonatas. As will be seen, it allows for a great deal of variety of proportion and detail:

First Part	*Second Part*
Main idea in the tonic key.	Main idea, or something akin to it, in related key, and

First Part contd.	*Second Part* contd.
	working back by a more or less adventurous route to the home-tonic.
Subsidiary idea in a related key (usually the dominant or relative minor).	Subsidiary idea in the tonic.

Each part played twice.

Of the following examples, those marked * will be found in *Classic Sonatas for Piano,* edited by Leo Podolsky (Fischer, New York), or scattered about various other collections.

Handel * The well-known *Fantasia* or *Sonata in C* (from the 3rd set of harpsichord lessons, no. 5).

Martini * *Sonata in E* (1st movement).
Sonata in F (1st and 2nd movements), quoted in full in Hadow's *Sonata Form* (Novello).

Galuppi * *Sonata in D.* A most instructive example. The 1st, 2nd and 4th movements may profitably be studied, but the 2nd is of particular interest.

Arne * The famous *Gigue in G* from the 6th of the '8 *sonatas or lessons*'.

Paradisi * *Sonata in A* (1st movement); a very highly-developed example.

J. C. Bach *Sonata op. X no. 2* for violin and piano, (1st movement).
Ditto no. 3, (1st movement). (These are published by Hinrichsen.)

Scarlatti Any volume containing some of D. Scarlatti's sonatas will certainly contain suitable examples.

The key-schemes of the two parts, each within itself and in relation to the whole, constitute one of the most important and significant facts in the history of Western European music. The tonal principles embodied in the examples just given, profoundly affected the thought that, even while J. S. Bach was in his prime, was being given by younger men to the question of further expansion. Of this we shall have something to say in the next part of this chapter. Meanwhile, it must surely be agreed that the 'open' 2-part scheme outlined above represents a high state of organisation of material and of key; though it is fairly obvious that it cannot be further expanded without losing coherence, unless some new principle is incorporated. That principle is to be found in the 'open 3-part form', whose relationship to the 2-part form which we have been discussing is, as was seen in chapter II, very close indeed.

2. *Transitional forms*

It is not possible to give a precise answer to the question when, or how, or at whose hands, the principle of recapitulating the *main* or first idea was introduced as a fundamental one in writing extended 'open' forms. It is certain that it was partly the result of deliberate experimenting on methods of progress; for it is clear that the younger contemporaries of J. S. Bach, including notably his son Carl Philipp Emmanuel, found the 2-part form cramping. Their works contain, besides many examples of the 2-part form pushed to (and sometimes beyond) the limits of coherence, numbers of experiments on various lines, and of differing degrees of success. One of the most interesting of these 'transitional' types is illustrated in a sonata of C. P. E. Bach (*Six sets of sonatas*, set 1, no. 2, 1st movement).

Ex. 10a

Ex. 10b

Ex. 10c

As will be seen from examples 10(a)—(c), the subsidiary idea of the first part is itself divided into two distinct parts, the first of which begins as a *transposition of the main idea into the dominant key*. Thus, upon the return to the tonic in the second part, one has the effect of recapitulation of the beginning of the first part, since both ideas begin alike. As a matter of fact, in this particular instance, the recapitulation is a kind of composite of the two ideas, ending up with a fairly exact statement of the latter part of the subsidiary idea. This example is also of particular interest in that it underlines the fact that contrast of key is more important than contrast of subject-matter; and it should be noted that it is a pointer to a frequent practice of Haydn's, which that master continued into his most mature work; namely, the starting of each 'subject' or 'group' of material with the same melody,[22] thus emphasising the principle of key-contrast which is the absolutely basic factor of all 'open' forms. Of the effects of various kinds of key-contrast more will be said in the next chapter.

C. P. E. Bach's instrumental works illustrate better than any others the transition from open 2-part form to the 'sonata form'. He himself never grasped the full implications of the task upon which he was engaged, and it was left to Haydn to establish the true principles of sonata form as such. Despite C. P. E. Bach's outspoken modernism, he showed a marked reluctance, or inability, to make a clean break with the past. None the less, his compositions are of crucial importance as illustrating every stage of the process of transition itself, and though copies of his works are a little less easily accessible than some other music, they are indispensible to the student who wishes to understand fully just what happened during the bridge-period between J. S. Bach and Mozart.

Other composers whose works are worthy of careful examination include J. C. Bach, Wm. Boyce, J. A. Hasse, Thomas Augustine Arne and Domenico Paradisi.[23] If the student can procure a copy of Arne's *8 Sonatas or Lessons for the Harpsichord* (published by Augener and others) he will

[22] See, for instance, the first movements of the following:—
Symphony no. 92 (the 'Oxford')
Symphony no. 104 (the 'London')
String quartet (op. 76 no. 3) (the 'Emperor')
The great *Pianoforte sonata in E flat* (*no. 1* in most editions)

[23] Instances are not wanting in the works of J. S. Bach himself; the 5th prelude in the 2nd book of the '48' affords a fine proof that the old man was not always conservative in these matters. It contains, in the passage from bar 41 to the end, the elements of recapitulation of both ideas in the tonic key; the essence of the matter is in the difference between bars 3-4 and bars 43-44. Similar in scope and design is the corrente in the E minor partita.

find the following movements of interest as showing the recapitulatory principle in various stages of completeness:

Rudimentary:

Sonata 1, 1st movement
Sonata 3, 2nd movement (Allegro)
Sonata 4, 1st movement
Sonata 4, last movement (after the fugue)
Sonata 7, last movement.

More advanced:

Sonata 5, Gavotte. (Of exceptional interest because of the manipulation of cadences in the first theme and its recapitulation, in order to achieve smooth key-transitions.)

Sonata 1, 2nd movement. (A very advanced example, being virtually a true sonata form on a small scale.)

(The Gigue from *Sonata 6* has already been cited as an advanced 2-part piece. The 3rd movement of *Sonata 2* is another.)

If possible, the student should compare Paradisi's well-known so-called *Toccata in A* (a transitional type) with the first movement of the sonata of which it is the finale.[24] The latter is probably as elaborate an example of the open 2-part form as ever achieved musical coherence; on the other hand, the same composer's *Sonata in D* (1st movement),[25] though of almost exactly the same length as the 1st movement of the *A major sonata,* is an open 3-part form of a considerably highly-developed kind. In passing, it is also of interest to note in this D major movement an attempt to increase interest, and to provide variety without sacrificing unity, by 'inverting' the main idea at the beginning of the second part.

Practically all the examples given in this chapter, including those exemplifying the emerging '3-part' principle, cling doggedly to the old formula of opening the second part with the main idea given in the dominant key. The disappearance

[24] Podolsky, *Classic Sonatas for Pianoforte,* p. 58.
[25] Ibid., p. 50.

of this predominance of the dominant just at this place in the design is one of the crucial final stages in the early history of the 'sonata form'. On the other hand, the even more important principle of key-adventuring in the second part, as old as the open forms themselves, becomes in the hands of Haydn and Beethoven, the medium of some of the most wonderful music ever written

V

THE SONATA FORM

THE PREVIOUS CHAPTER traced the gradual evolution of the 'open' forms up to the point at which the time was ripe for Haydn and Mozart to bring their genius to bear upon them, and to perfect the 'sonata form', one of the most thoroughly satisfactory vehicles for the conveyance of musical ideas. It seems clear that the 'transitional' composers, finding it impossible to expand further on the 2-part principle, turned gradually to the 3-part one in their need to find a logical means of developing the art of music, and it is perfectly natural that, so far as possible, they incorporated the old proved principles in their work. While it is impossible to draw a clear dividing line between 'old' and 'new' at any point during the transitional period, it is quite clear that Haydn and Mozart brought a radical new factor into the situation: what, following Tovey's lead, we may call the 'sonata style'.

The essential difference between the 'rhetorical' and the 'sonata' styles lies in the method by which unity of design is achieved. The rhetorical movement depends upon long stretches of unbroken mood, of uninterrupted flow of musical idea; it enlarges upon a single topic, and achieves unity through never departing from that topic, developing by what Bukofzer calls 'continuous expansion'.[26] On the other hand, the sonata style is dramatic, in that its object is to bring into play contrasted and even opposed ideas, whose interplay and whose reactions to one another provide the interest of the music; and it is the composer's task to achieve unity by making his varied material coalesce; that is, by reconciling and resolving the conflicting and contrasting elements.

[26] *Music in the Baroque Era*, p. 287.

During the transitional period, music was expanding in several directions, each of which had to play a necessary part in the formation of the 'sonata style', and Haydn was the composer to whom it fell to bring together for the first time all the necessary ingredients. He grasped almost from the start the *dramatic* value of the contrast and opposition of two keys which had grown up as a natural function of the melodic development of the small open forms. In his work it is clearly shown that the contrast of two tonalities, and their ultimate reconciliation, is the fundamental basis of the sonata form; a fact which is clearly demonstrated in his frequent habit (which actually grew *more* frequent) of beginning both his groups of thematic material with the same melody, but in contrasted keys. Formally, such a proceeding is a link with the past, and we have shown (page 57) that in C. P. E. Bach's work it is actually one of the most important links in the chain of development; but until Haydn made a dramatic point of it, it was scarcely more than a reflection of past influence upon modern method.[27]

The subsequent history of sonata form is really divisible into two stages: (1) the organisation of the *material* contained in the contrasted key-groups and (2) the expansion of the whole system of key-relationships to embrace the entire range of tonality made possible by equal temperament, instead of the restricted circle of keys which fulfilled the requirements of an earlier age. Haydn, Mozart and Beethoven are all concerned in the first of these stages; on the other hand, it is perhaps Beethoven's chief claim to greatness that his work on the second stage was to lay down principles which underlie most of the great instrumental music which has been written since, and which, when they have been challenged by composers such as Liszt, have in the end reasserted themselves triumphantly.

The name 'sonata form', though illogical as it is generally

[27] See list on page 58, f.n. 22. This feature is occasionally found in Mozart also; see for example the first movements of the piano sonatas K.570 and K.576.

applied, has the advantage over the expressions 'binary' and 'ternary' that everybody is agreed as to what it stands for. For this reason, and because it is concise and handy, we shall continue to use it, rather than 'developed open 3-part form' or 'compound open 3-part form', which, though more accurate, do not have these recommendations. Let us make an unadorned drawing of the skeleton, whose relationship to skeletons drawn in earlier chapters will be quite clear:

Introduction (optional)	1 *(Exposition)*	2 *(Development)*	3 *(Recapitulation)*	Coda (optional)
	(A) 1st group of material in tonic key.	A digression into keys not hitherto emphasised; using material either from (1) or, more rarely, new; or both; and leading back to the edge of the original tonic key.	(A) 1st group of material, again in the tonic key.	
	Link, or transitional passage leading to the edge of the new key.		Transitional passage modified in some way so as *not* to lead away from the home-key.	
	(B) 2nd group of material in a related key.		(B) 2nd group of material, this time in the home-key.	
	Repeat of (1)[28]		(Rarely) Repeat of (2) and (3).[28]	

By way of illustration of these anatomical generalities, we now take a movement from each of the three great classical composers, indicating the main sections only. The student is advised to follow these carefully, and then to practise making similar broad analyses:

Note: Henceforth the expressions '1st part' and '2nd part' are dropped, in favour of the universally-accepted 'exposition' 'development' and 'recapitulation'.

[28] The repeats are obviously a survival from the smaller 'open' forms, and are seldom played. The second repeat (that of [2] and [3]), though occasionally found in print as late as middle Beethoven (see his piano sonata op. 57, finale), was virtually abandoned soon after sonata-form was well-established. The first, though surviving in some works so late as the symphonies of Brahms and Dvorak, was often omitted by Beethoven and subsequently.

Mozart—Pianoforte sonata in F (K.332), 1st movement.

Introduction	None.
Exposition	(A) First group, bars 1-22.
	Transition, bars 23-40.
	(B) Second group in the dominant key, bars 41-93.
	Exposition repeated.
Development	New or 'episodical' material bars 94-109.
	Based on part of the 2nd group bars 109-132.
Recapitulation	(A) First group in tonic, bars 133-154.
	Modified transition bars 155-176.
	(B) Second group in the tonic key bars 177-229.
Coda	None.
	Repeat from development to end.

Haydn—Pianoforte sonata in C, 1st movement (No. 5 in all standard editions).

Introduction	None.
Exposition	(A) First group bars 1-20.
	Transition bars 20-35.
	(B) Second group centred on the dominant key, bars 26-67, including a closing-section or 'codetta' based on the 1st group, at bars 62-67.
	Repeat of exposition.
Development	Bars 68-103.
Recapitulation	(A) 1st group bars 104-111 (cf. exposition).
	Modified transition 112-125.
	(B) 2nd group centred on the tonic, bars 126-151, omitting the closing-section.
Coda	Bars 152-170.
	Repeat of development, recapitulation and coda.

Beethoven—Pianoforte sonata in C minor, op. 13, 1st movement.

Introduction	10 bars.
Exposition	(A) 1st group bars 1-25, closing into
	Transition bars 25-40, closing into
	(B) 2nd group bars 41-122, at first in the mediant minor, thereafter in the mediant (or 'relative') major.
	Repeat of exposition.
Development	Bars 123-184 closing into
Recapitulation	(A) 1st group, bars 185-197.
	Transition (quite different) bars 197-210.
	(B) 2nd group at first in the subdominant, thereafter in tonic, bars 211-284.
Coda	Bars 285-300.

The following movements are suitable for practice on similar lines: (in each case the 1st movement of the work named.)

Haydn	*Pianoforte sonata in D* (Augener no. 7: Peters no. 7[29])
	Pianoforte sonata in F (Augener no. 13: Peters no. 21[29])
Mozart	*Pianoforte sonata in F (K.280).*
	Pianoforte sonata in C (K.309).
	Pianoforte sonata in A minor (K.310).
	Pianoforte sonata in B flat (K.333).
	Symphony in E flat, no. 39.
	Symphony in G minor, no. 40.
	Symphony in C, no. 41.
Beethoven	*Pianoforte sonata in F minor (op. 2 no. 1)*
	Pianoforte sonata in D (op. 10 no. 3)
	Pianoforte sonata in G (op. 14 no. 2)
	Pianoforte sonata in B flat (op. 22)
	Pianoforte sonata in D (op. 28)
	Pianoforte sonata in C (op. 53)
	Pianoforte sonata in E minor (op. 90)
	Symphony no. 1 in C.
	Symphony no. 2 in D.
	Symphony no. 4 in B flat.

At this stage, the student is advised to concentrate upon the broad formal lines of all the classical chamber and symphonic music he can hear; it will not be long before he realises that no special gifts are required to follow the trend of the composer's design, and in particular he will quickly learn to recognise the recapitulation when he hears it, and to appreciate the subtleties of the varying relationships between the principal keys. It cannot be too strongly stated that the power to do this is *not* confined to the small number of people possessing 'absolute pitch', for since the composer's design relies upon these features, he has failed in his task if he does not make them clear to all attentive listeners.

Superficial analysis of the sort so far employed provides useful practice in musical anatomy, and is all very well in its way. It can be applied successfully to hundreds of movements, not only by Haydn, Mozart and Beethoven, and their successors Schubert, Mendelssohn, Brahms and so on (not to speak

[29] References to Peters edition of Haydn's sonatas are to the newer edition by Martienssen, unless otherwise stated.

of such later masters as Elgar, Sibelius and Vaughan Williams), but also to even greater numbers of the works of the forgotten Spohr, Dussek, Ries, Hummel, Rubinstein, and scores of still smaller fry.

We are therefore faced with the question of what it is that differentiates between the great and the insignificant. Is it the greater beauty of the melodies? No, because it is demonstrable that the works of the lesser men contain many beautiful tunes, whereas Beethoven can write magnificent movements like the 1st movement of the 'Waldstein' sonata (op. 53), using melodic material which in isolation from its context appears to be commonplace and uninteresting. Is it facility and smoothness of workmanship? No, because if it were, Mendelssohn would outshine Beethoven. Is it originality of harmony? No, because it is apparent that in this respect Spohr was at least as great an innovator as Beethoven. It would be hard to find anybody who would not agree that such comparisons are ludicrous, and that Haydn's, Mozart's, and Beethoven's works demonstrate their superiority at every turn.

This brings us back to the 'sonata style', for the difference between Beethoven and Hummel (for instance) lies chiefly in the fact that the former was a master of the style, while the latter was unaware of its existence, if the evidence of his decorative compositions is to be relied upon. The great masters, in fact, had complete command of the sonata style; their music is a continuous demonstration of the fact that during the transition from Bach to Haydn, the main emphasis in music had shifted to its dramatic, as opposed to its rhetorical, functions. Every aspect of the classical masters' music shows this change of emphasis: the emergence of the sonata-form: the relative recession of pure counterpoint in favour of increased harmonic interest for its own sake: the new type of opera developed by Gluck to replace the older 'concerts in fancy-dress': the beginnings of orchestration on modern lines, and the development of the instruments which made it possible. The sonata style is a style of composition in which all these factors are assimilated in the composer's handling of conflict, contrast and resolution.

A textbook of musical design is not the place to enlarge upon questions of style, and the reader who wishes (as he ought to wish) to follow these matters up, is referred in the first instance to the writings of Sir Donald Tovey and Sir Hubert Parry, and to the music discussed in them. But certain aspects of style are completely bound up with the treatment of the sonata form by Haydn, Mozart and Beethoven, and require to be examined.

The Exposition.

At the risk of boring the reader, we state again that he must never forget that the sonata style, being essentially a dramatic one, involves, of necessity, contrasts of mood, contrasts of emotional temperature; and it is thus that the juxtaposition of key-centres or tonics assumes so great an importance. To give the maximum effect to this juxtaposition, the material is ordered into two tonally-contrasted groups or 'subjects'; the word 'subject', formerly universally used in this connection, has been largely superseded by the much more accurate 'group', which conveys far more realistically the real nature of the exposition; for the 'groups' are of no fixed size, and have no settled characteristics except that of clearly fixing their respective keys. The *first group* more often than not consists of a single musical idea; but it may contain two (Mozart, *Piano sonata K. 332*) or three (Beethoven, *Piano sonata op. 90*), and there is no absolute law which would prevent it having more. The *second group,* on the other hand, rarely consists of less than two distinct ideas, and usually of more; sometimes, particularly in the hands of Beethoven and Brahms, it takes the form of a huge parade of themes, perhaps half-a-dozen or more, as for instance in the first movements of Beethoven's pianoforte sonatas *op. 7* and *op. 28,* or of his *3rd Symphony.*

As we have seen, the first idea of the second group may (in Haydn often, in Mozart occasionally, in Beethoven never), open with the same phrase as does the first group. The *last* is normally of such a kind as to give, very properly, the impression of rounding-off an important part of the design; very often, but not at all necessarily, it harks back to some earlier idea, usually from the first group (Mozart, *K. 310;* Beethoven, *op. 13*). Confusion has arisen through the use of the word 'codetta' to describe this section, different restrictions being laid down by different authorities; since the word has an undisputed implication in connection with the *fugue,* we have preferred to avoid it altogether so far as the sonata form is concerned, and to refer to it as the 'closing-section'.

We must realise that the composer has to arrange the tonal- or key-relationship of his groups, one to another, in such a way that the move from the first key-centre to the second is felt to be in the direction of increased action or emotional impetus, as befits the gradual revealing of the elements of a dramatic plot; and it is this fact which accounts for the universal use of the dominant or the relative major key for the second group, during the earlier history of the mature form; for experience of music from the earliest times since the major and minor scales were established shows that these particular shifts of key-centre (from a major tonic to its dominant, and from a minor tonic to its mediant) have just this effect; the effect which Tovey describes as a 'step up'. The unsatisfactory nature of the opposite move (i.e. to the sub-dominant, etc. is simply explained when we realise that any given key *is* the dominant of its own sub-dominant, and therefore the relationship is as of a psychological step *down.* Whatever the cause, these are the demonstrable effects, and such attempts as have been made to try the sub-dominant as the main key-centre of the second group do result in an effect of enervation or emotional recession, just when it is not wanted.[30]

Examination of the works of the three great classical

[30] The student is referred to Prout's *Applied Forms,* paragraphs 240-247, for a summary of the position as regards keys for the second group.

masters shows that this tonic-dominant or tonic-relative major relationship as between the first and second groups preponderates; indeed, with Haydn and Mozart it is almost universal. Beethoven, while commonly accepting the general rule, organised the relations of one key to another more systematically and thoroughly, and as his work progressed, tended more and more to exploit the new dramatic effects of hitherto unused relationships. He, and Brahms following him, show a marked predilection for the mediant and sub-mediant in relation to an established major tonic (see Beethoven *op. 31 no. 1, op. 53, op. 106,* first movements) and for the dominant in relation to an established minor tonic (Beethoven *op. 31 no. 2, op. 90*), and they occasionally employ still more unexpected juxtapositions. (See also, for example, the first movements of Brahms' *2nd, 3rd* and *4th Symphonies*.)

Note, as a vital related fact, that the important element being the contrast of *main key-centres,* it is possible for the composer, having established his second key, to diverge from it temporarily; the effect, in a properly managed case, is, paradoxically, to confirm the sense of contrast given by the main juxtaposition of keys, by throwing the second key into increased relief. A striking case in point is the first movement of Haydn's well-known *Emperor quartet in C major (op. 76 no. 3).* Here, the second group in G is interrupted by a dark and morose section in E flat major at bars 33-36. The triumphant effect of the re-establishment of the orthodox dominant key throws an almost melodramatic light upon the main action. Such mastery of drama is not to be confused with the somewhat aimless tonal wanderings which disfigure much of Schubert's large-scale work.

There remains for consideration the transition. Since its main function is to *lead* satisfactorily from one key to the threshold of another, we need not be surprised to find great variety of method and of material used by the masters. The most frequently found external forms taken by Beethoven (who may stand as example for the others) in his transitions are as follow:

(1) Starting with matter from the opening theme and diverging. (See the 1st movements of *op. 7; op. 14 no. 1; op. 22; op. 49 no. 1; op. 53.)*

(2) Entirely based on material drawn from the first group. (See the 1st movements of *op. 2 no. 1; op. 10 no. 2; op. 10 no. 3; op. 13; op. 31 nos. 1* and *2*)

(3) Entirely new as regards thematic material. (See the 1st movements of *op. 10 no. 1; op. 14 no. 2; op. 28*)

(4) Starting with new material and reverting to old. (See the 1st movement of *op. 31 no. 3).*

(5) Forecasting some part of the 2nd group. (See the first movements of *op. 2 nos. 2* and *3).*

In short, so far as its thematic content is concerned, the transition may be long or short, loud or soft, new or old, significant or formal, being governed only by the composer's understanding of the needs of the particular situation; it must provide a spring-board for the key of the second group; it must *not* interfere with the opposition of the two main key-centres, and must therefore never settle down too firmly in any new key, though it may pass momentarily in and out of several. Once arrived at the threshold (which usually means the dominant) of the new key, it may pause for breath *(op. 49 no. 2)* or poise itself (as in most Beethoven movements) or it may flow into the second group without interruption *(op. 53);* the circumstances and the nature of the material dictate such matters, about which there can be no hard-and-fast rules, since they are not anatomical facts, but the very life of the music itself.[31]

We may conveniently pause here for a moment to consider

[31] An interesting form of transition is that which remains throughout in the tonic key, finishing on the dominant chord. The second group starts without further ado in the new key, by regarding this same chord as a tonic. Upon recapitulation, no modification of the transition is required, since the second group follows perfectly naturally by taking the dominant chord in its true character as a dominant. This method is found in Haydn and earlier composers such as J. C. Bach, but was particularly beloved by Mozart, in whose music examples abound. See, for example, the first movements of his piano sonatas *K.280, 281, 283, 284, 545,* and string quartets *K.575, 590.* Also Haydn's *pianoforte sonata no. 7* and J. C. Bach's sonatas for violin and piano, *op. X nos. 2* and *5.*

briefly what constitutes 'settling into a new key'. Tovey has written in several different volumes of the difference between being '*on* the dominant' and '*in* the dominant', and for a full exposition of the subject, the reader is referred to his works.[32]

The main point is that the rule-of-thumb which states that a key is established when its dominant and tonic have been sounded in succession will not meet the facts of the sonata-exposition, however useful it may be for the determining of the keys of isolated passages without their context. Normally, when a key is well established, emphasis or reiteration of a major chord outside that key will arouse the sensation of expectancy or unrest; now, it is the chief characteristic of a dominant chord that it engenders just this kind of mental anticipation, a desire to move which is gratified at the point where the tonic is sounded. Thus it is that the many cases occurring towards the end of the transition sections of classical sonata forms, of reiteration of the supertonic major chord, do not *sound* (however much they may look in print) like established tonics, but like dominants of the dominant key: what Tovey calls 'enhanced dominants'. It is a fact easily verifiable by experiment that it is not possible within the classical harmonic framework to establish a direct relationship between a key and the major key of its own supertonic; for so strong is the tonic-dominant instinct that the supertonic major chord, no matter how much it may be surrounded and hedged-in by its own family, will always sound as if it were about to lead to something else. To *modulate* from C major to D major is not impossible, but it can be done convincingly only by first destroying all feeling of C major; in which case, no relationship can be said to exist between the two keys. Among the easiest examples to follow is that instanced by Tovey, viz. bars 19-25 of the first movement of Beethoven's *Pianoforte sonata op. 14 no. 2* which, isolated from their context, may well sound as if they were in A major. When the movement is listened to atten-

[32] *Beethoven* pp. 13-15; *Companion to Beethoven's pianoforte sonatas* pp. 6-7, etc.

tively from the start, however, they arouse no settled feelings at all, but only expectancy for that which occurs at bar 26—the chord of D major. In other words, despite *appearances* to the contrary, those A major chords were not tonic, but dominant.

The companion sonata, *op. 14 no. 1,* provides at bars 17-22 another easily-followed example, and further cases in point are numerous, particularly among the symphonic and chamber works of Beethoven. More often than not, however, there is no conflict between the sound and the appearance of the printed page.

Bearing all this in mind, let us now have a closer look at our three examples, and make a more detailed analysis of their expositions:

Mozart, K. 332, 1st movement, exposition.

First Group:

A(i)	Bars 1-12, theme consisting of a sentence of three 4-bar phrases in the key of F.
A(ii)	Bars 13-22, new theme in two 4-bar phrases with extension by two repetitions of the cadence.
Transition	Bars 23-40. A plunge into D minor, and a completely new theme. Two 4-bar phrases, followed by thrice 2 bars passing through C minor and leading to 4 bars affirmation of the chord of G (i.e., the dominant of the dominant key.)

Second Group:

B(i)	Bars 41-56. An 8-bar sentence in C major (the dominant), coming to a half-close and repeated with melodic embellishments and modified to reach a full-close. Overlapping into:
B(ii)	Bars 56-70. New theme starting in C major and changing to C minor at bar 58, whence it moves via E flat back to the dominant of C, upon which it leans for 4 bars. This theme, it should be noted, is of a dark, dramatic nature, more notable for its rhythmic and harmonic qualities than for melodic beauty.
B(iii)	Bars 71-86. A quiet new theme in C major, consisting of a 6-bar phrase repeated in a higher octave, and closing into twice two bars affirming the cadence.

B(iv) Closing theme, bars 87-93. Essentially a series of cadential formalities, in 2 plus 2 plus 3 bars.

Haydn, Piano sonata no. 5 in C major, 1st movement, exposition.

FIRST GROUP:

A Bars 1-20. One theme only; an 8-bar sentence with full close, repeated with slight embellishment and closing into four bars prolongation of the cadence over a tonic pedal, closing into:

Transition Bars 20-35, arising from the three repeated notes of bar 1 and developed to bar 26, whence the figure of bars 5-6 is taken up, leading to a chord of D major (enhanced dominant') at bar 32, which is reaffirmed for 4 bars.

SECOND GROUP:

B(i) Bars 36-45. New theme in G (the dominant), coming to a full close.

B(ii) Bars 46-62. A 5-bar phrase including reference to the repeated-note figure from bar 1 of the first group, followed by development of same in embellished form to an inverted full-close in the dominant at bar 60, with repetition of the last two bars.

B(iii) Bars 62-67. Closing theme consisting of four confirmatory full-closes using the prevailing rhythmic formulae.

Beethoven, Piano sonata in C minor, op. 13, exposition.

Introduction: 10 bars in very slow tempo, enunciating an important figure in bar 1; developing it and coming to a pause on the dominant.

FIRST GROUP:

A Bars 1-25. A single theme consisting of a 9-bar sentence with full close, overlapping self-repetition with modifications, to end in a half-close; followed by twice 4 bars on the dominant, closing into:

Transition Bars 25-40, based on the main figure of the first group, and moving in four-bar phrases, with pedal B flat (dominant of the relative major) from bar 33.

SECOND GROUP:

B(i) Bars 41-78 in E flat minor (!), passing through D flat (57), E flat minor again (69), F minor (73), C minor (75) and reaching towards the orthodox E flat major at 77. Closing into:

B(ii) Bars 79-102. New theme of 12 bars repeated.

B(iii) Closing theme, bars 103-122, of 4 bars repeated, leading into 4 confirmatory bars based upon the 1st group over a tonic pedal; then, over a bass falling one step each bar, reaching the dominant of G minor. For the repeat of the exposition this is at once followed by the dominant of the home-tonic; for the continuation into the development section it leads into the expected G minor.

After following the above analyses in detail, the student should do similar work for himself, choosing first of all examples from the list on page 65.

The Development

The development section of a sonata form is, like the second act of a play, the proper place for dramatic action, for the introduction of the unexpected, the exciting incident; for the shedding of new light upon the subjects of the drama by their behaviour in such situations; and not least for the creating, towards its end, of a special situation which will lead to the *dénouement* which is the recapitulation (or third act).

As the middle section of a simple 'open' 3-part form digressed from the firm tonal scheme of the first section, ranging more widely in key and gradually arousing a desire for a return to the safety and solidity of the tonic, so, in its more complex way, does the development section in a sonata form perform the same office on a larger scale. The *principle* of the development section is that it shall provide adventure and suspense.

The customary view is that it gives the composer opportunities to display his skill in manipulating his material. Textbooks are wont to give lists of the methods which may be employed, such as alteration of the mode: variation of the harmony, accompaniment or rhythm: contrapuntal treatment, and so on. All these, while doubtless important in their way, are no more than the technical means to the end which is too often given inadequate treatment by theorists;

analysis of such *means* is only a matter of observation of that which can be seen upon the surface, and can be carried out without any understanding of the underlying musical *action*. The proper view, and that which is in line with the historical evolution of the form, is that the development provides the opportunity for *tonal digressions,* that is, for ventures into keys or tonalities more or less remote from the tonic; for adventure and exploration contrasting with the stability of the firmly-rooted exposition; and that these tonal digressions are carried through as a rule by manipulation of some of the material of the exposition; though there is nothing to prevent all or part of the section being episodical, i.e., based upon quite fresh musical matter, and in fact, such was a favourite method with Mozart. Beethoven's works also contain several outstanding cases of episodes introduced into the development section, the most notable being in the first movement of his third symphony, in which a passage of completely new material occurs twice (contrary to the arbitrary definition of an episode given in some text-books). We must be very careful to repel any suggestion that there are rules governing what a composer may or may not do with his material; his only criterion, as usual, is that of suitability to the particular circumstances of the piece of music in hand. At one end of the scale we have Mozart with his perfectly-proportioned but often episodical development sections, while at the other there are movements like the finale of Dvořák's *'New World' symphony,* which comes near to ruin through the composer's over-elaborate display of ingenuity in the combination of themes from different movements of the work. Beethoven seldom fails to make the most of his development, and often (as e.g., in the 1st movements of the piano sonatas *op. 28* and *53*) uses minute and apparently trifling little figures to work up passages of tremendous drama and passion. Real development consists far more in such use of significant fragments as vehicles for tonal adventures than in 'playing in E major what has already been heard in C major'.

We shall, in fact, not be wrong if we adopt the standpoint that our first duty in the study of development is to follow out the composer's key-scheme, with particular attention to his method of return to his home-tonic. Analysis of the actual themes used, and of the manner of their treatment, are, if not unimportant, at least secondary to this. Whether the composer's method is elaborate or simple, whether episodical or derivatory, whether he sticks to one theme or ranges widely over his material, are matters of detail to be studied and analysed within the larger framework laid down by the scope and nature of the individual work.

It is often said that in the works of Haydn and Mozart, the art of development is shown in its infancy, and that it was left to Beethoven to exploit its possibilities fully. This is not merely misleading in its implication that Haydn's and Mozart's music shows less mastery of the technique of composition, and in its suggestion that the material and proportions of their compositions could have borne development in Beethoven's manner, but it is also literally untrue. Both Haydn and Mozart are perfectly capable of holding their own in any company where matters of ingenuity, variety, dramatic tension and suspense on a large scale are in question. It was part of their genius that they knew just when and to what extent such characteristics were in keeping with the music they were writing. If Haydn is as a rule more adventurous than Mozart, and Mozart more exquisitely polished than Haydn, that is only a reflection of their individual solutions of the problems of their art. That Beethoven's main contribution to the sonata-form was to expand it in every direction (including its tonal range, and therefore the scope and consequently the means of the development section) in no way affects the perfection of Haydn's and Mozart's achievements, nor does it lessen the complete effectiveness of their own methods of development.

Let us now examine the developments of our three examples:

Mozart, K.332:

The tonal scheme consists of the time-honoured progress from the dominant through a number of keys to the threshold of the tonic; the scheme usually found in the early 'open' forms. In this case C major (the dominant) holds sway for the entire length (bars 94-109) of a square little episode of one 8-bar sentence repeated. The music next proceeds to develop the rhythmic figure enunciated in the second theme of the second group (Bii), passing into C minor, thence via G minor (115) and D minor (119) to a half-close in the latter key at 123. There follow 4 bars affirmation of the cadence, based on the figure of bars 67-8 from the same theme, and a switch thence at bar 129 to the dominant chord of the home-key, a move of such simplicity that its effectiveness as a dramatic stroke is cause for amazement. We are now almost home, and a further three bars of dominant preparation (i.e., sound of the home-dominant) take us to the end of the section, whence the recapitulation follows with ease and naturalness.

Haydn, sonata no. 5:

Unlike Mozart in the example just examined, Haydn in this instance is using the development chiefly as a means of stressing the flat, or subdominant side of his home-key. Since the home-key *is* the dominant of its own subdominant, we may expect that the return home will give the same mental effect of a step up which is usually associated with all moves to the sharp side; and this is indeed the case. At bars 68-71 we have a phrase developed from bars 5-6 of the first group, clearly designed to lead us away from the dominant key which has been our centre of operations for so long, since it makes a half-close on the dominant of the relative minor key. Clearly, then, we are all set to move away in this key (A minor). Haydn, however, has different ideas, and with characteristic audacity, he plunges into the subdominant key (F) instead, and proceeds to give us the entire main sentence of the first group in that key, using the repeat version of bars 9-16 with its triplet accompaniment. These triplets (inverted and taken to the top of the harmony), now become the main thematic feature of the rest of the development, in a long modulatory passage whose absence of melodic features is not a weakness, but a proof that tonal considerations are of leading interest. Passing through G (82), it reaches the spurned A minor at 83, and works its way back by a series of inconclusive steps from 87, to F major again at the end of 89. Yet another attempt to establish A minor is made, starting over a pedal E at bar 94; but it is now too late for anything decisive in that line, and a couple of bars of great harmonic beauty lead us to the edge of D minor. Three more bars, and we are pausing on the home-dominant; and so to the recapitulation.

Beethoven, op. 13:

This section, though little if any longer than the others already examined, is part of a work whose melodramatic quality is thoroughly characteristic of Beethoven, and outside the ordinary emotional range of Haydn or Mozart; appropriately, it contains melodramatic features which would be entirely out of place in either of the works already discussed.

It begins by proceeding to G minor, to give us the opening two bars of the *introduction*. In two more bars, by means of the kind of equivocation known as an 'enharmonic modulation' we are landed miles away in E minor, and all sense of our original stable tonal foundations is lost to us. Beethoven has now to take us back home again, and resuming the interrupted *allegro*, he proceeds to alternate the figure of the first 2 bars of the first group with the main figure of the introduction, now in quick time. From 133-157 he avoids any settled tonality, and after 139 abandons the second of his two figures, finally allowing his material (like his tonality) to disintegrate. He has looked at (without reaching) G minor, F, C, and F again, and finally lands on the chord of G.

This chord, of course, is our home dominant; but after what has passed we are not likely to recognise it as such, and Beethoven now proceeds to provide circumstantial evidence that we are on the doorstep of our home. For no fewer than 28 bars he insists upon this G major harmony, now moving momentarily from the G bass only to return immediately with greater insistence; now introducing the 7th and 9th of the chord; now hinting at the C minor harmony to come; in fact, using all manner of devices to arouse in our minds the expectation of a great event impending. If that great event be not the return home, what shall it be? Well, Beethoven had not by op. 13 reached the stage when (as he later did in the 4th symphony) he was prepared to go to elaborate lengths such as this, only to play a great hoax; it is the home-dominant all right, as we gratefully recognise when, after the tension has reached its climax at bar 177, an 8-bar run (still on the dominant) takes us flying into the tonic key and the recapitulation of the first group.

The rather spectacular way in which, in the example just analysed, Beethoven makes his return to his home key and to the recapitulation of his thematic material, draws attention to this crucial point in the progress of any movement in sonata form. It is scarcely an exaggeration to say that in all sonata forms this last part of the development is the supremely critical point, and that failure to manage it adequately can wreck an otherwise well-written movement.

The root of the matter lies, of course, in arriving at the 'threshold' of the home-tonic key, which, at least until Beethoven's maturity, in practice means its dominant. The 'preparation' which may take place once the dominant is reached, is a matter closely allied to the general emotional quality of the movement as a whole, and it can be broadly affirmed that the longer the 'preparation' lasts, the greater the excitement and anticipation which is aroused in the listener's mind, and the greater the sense of relief or satisfaction brought about by the actual return to the first group. Thus the long stretch of dominant preparation in the first movement of Beethoven's *'Waldstein' sonata* (bars 142-155) creates a steadily-mounting tension which reaches a point of fury at the downward rush which leads into the tonic chord; a state of affairs which is underlined and increased by the skill with which Beethoven manages his material and by the long slow crescendo over the whole passage. Beethoven's peculiar mastery in these matters, however, lies more in the dramatic strokes by which he turns his tonality round from the most unlikely directions to the home dominant; strokes which are sometimes so swift and unexpected as to leave the listener gasping, and only too grateful if the composer gives him a little time to regain his bearings. Consider for a moment bars 109-139 of the first movement of the *'Appassionata' sonata (op. 57).* At bar 109 the composer is in the full flight of his development, and the music has just settled into D flat major, a relative of the tonic F minor. The composer proceeds to develop the first phrase of the 'second group' in that key, moving at 114 to B flat minor, then quickly through G flat major, into B minor, which is about as remote from the home-tonic as it is possible to be. The harmony then proceeds to disintegrate, the music flying down the keyboard on one of those equivocal chords which lie behind so many of Beethoven's master-strokes, to emerge on the other side (bar 134) on a reiterated bass C natural, *over which,* as a dominant pedal, the recapitulation in the tonic key begins.

By no means all recapitulations are brought about in so dramatic a fashion as this; but then, few movements rise to the heights of passion where such strokes would be in place. Nevertheless, a clear understanding of the importance of this feature, and a knowledge of the methods adopted by the greatest composers in handling it, are among the absolutely indispensible elements of a musical education, and the student is advised to spend a great deal of time in examining 'approaches' to recapitulation. Beethoven, in his second and third periods, and Brahms and other composers following him, have demonstrated that there are other and subtler ways of returning home than by elaborate dominant preparation. Allusion has been made to his 4th symphony in which great trouble is taken to make the listener believe that he is on the threshold of the home-tonic, only to lead to a dramatic revelation that he was nothing of the sort. Examination of the 1st movements of the pianoforte sonatas *op. 81a, op. 90, op. 101, op. 106* and *op. 110* will reveal equally subtle, though entirely different, methods of approach.

A more recent composer who shows a very firm grasp of the importance of this matter of the return home is Sibelius. His first five symphonies all contain cases in point, which demonstrate both the method of arousing an accumulating sense of expectancy (the finale of the 2nd symphony gives us one of the most hair-raising examples of this method in all music), and that of obscuring the issue so as to make the clarification all the more welcome (as in the 1st movement of the 4th).

Careful study of the analyses given on pages 77-78, followed by the student's own work upon the development sections of other works from our list, will provide a sound basis for understanding the endless subtleties and (where appropriate) ingenuities of the great composers' methods of development of their material. In an introductory book of this kind it is not possible, much as one would wish to do it, to follow out in detail more than a few examples. One would like to demonstrate how, in the 1st movements of his *4th* and *7th symphonies*, Beethoven creates subtle psychological connections between his development sections and the long slow introductions which have preceded the movements proper, and whose import cannot be fully appreciated until these connections have been established. One would like to proceed step by step through the tremendous finale of Brahms's 1st symphony, and a score of other movements, each one of which would provide fresh evidence of the inexhaustibility of the artistry of such composers; the student must learn to find these for himself; if he will proceed on the lines indicated, and arm himself with Tovey's *Essays in Musical Analysis* to help him to see the light more quickly and more vividly, he will be well rewarded.

The Recapitulation

It must be clear to the student by this time that the æsthetic effect of the recapitulation is to restore the emotional balance of the movement by providing stability and security after the tonally adventurous middle section. To this end, a complete restatement of the material as set out in the exposition, but now centred throughout on the home-tonic, is seldom felt to be too much, though plenty of cases occur in which this plan is modified. Straightforward cases of perfectly balanced orthodox recapitulation are the rule in Mozart and Beethoven, to which exceptions are found in modifications of detail, shortenings, even in the omission of whole sections. Haydn, on the other hand, is much freer in his treatment of this part of the sonata form; he frequently diverges radically from the order of events as set out in his expositions, especially in his later works; indeed, some of his most mature 'recapitulations' are really rather in the nature of fantasias upon some of the material of his expositions; keeping strictly to the tonic key, but having distinct qualities of 'summing-up' rather than of 'restatement', and akin, perhaps, to the highly-developed codas of Beethoven's middle and late periods. Such is the 1st movement of his *Pianoforte sonata in C sharp minor (no. 6)*, and another easily accessible example is the 1st movement of the 'Oxford' symphony.

These differences amount to no more than illustrations of the individual approach of different men of genius to the same problem, that of creating in the mind of the listener the feeling of satisfaction in the successful completion of a process. It is worth drawing attention to the one technical point upon which all depends, viz., the obvious fact that (except in the special case described in the footnote on page 70) the *transition* must differ, at least in detail, from the original as given in the exposition. More often than not, the difference consists simply of a modification of some small feature, to allow of a natural continuation in the tonic, instead of the dominant key.[33] Such is the case in our Mozart example (K.332); comparison of bars 155-176 with bars 23-40 will show that a sequential process in the middle has the desired effect. In our Haydn and Beethoven examples, on the other hand, the process is more elaborate. In the Haydn, the original transition gives place to what seems to be a restatement of the first group in the tonic minor. After a few bars, however, this is linked to the latter part of the original transition, now a fifth lower than before, and hence leading naturally to the second group in the tonic. Somewhat similarly, Beethoven in the op. 13 movement abandons his former scheme of transition, and now leads out of his first group into his second by a process of sequential development of his first theme. We may deduce from these examples that in this, as in other respects, there is no restraint upon the composer save his sense of what is fitting in the peculiar local situation. It is not for Beethoven to conform to preconceived regulations, but for us to learn from his practice.

[33] Attention is drawn to the remarkable example of the first movement of Beethoven's *5th symphony*, where an apparently insignificant enharmonic change in one chord makes the necessary modification, as the very simply managed sequel shows. Compare bars 52-58 with bars 296-302.

It is scarcely necessary for us to say more about the technique of recapitulation, nor of its æsthetics, save to draw attention to Tovey's remarks[34] as to the deceptiveness of supposing it to be a mechanical method of achieving symmetry. On the contrary, it has the function fundamental to any highly organised work of art, of unifying that which was diverse.

The Coda

Coda is the name given to all that part of the movement which remains after the recapitulation is completed. It is, like the introduction, an entirely optional part of any movement, though it is rare for a work of any size from Beethoven's time onwards to be without one. It had its origins, without doubt, in the desire of composers to reinforce their final cadences by repetition, and by extra emphasis upon the tonic chord. Thus the end of the work could be made more imposing, and could be differentiated from the ends of mere sections. Speaking on the whole, Mozart's codas are of this nature, even in his mature works; for example, in twelve important sonata movements in the last six big symphonies (nos. 35, 36, 38-41) one finds no coda at all in three: a purely formal coda in five; and a more highly-organised coda only in four. Of these last four, those in the finales of symphonies nos. 35 and 41 are the only ones that can be said to be on a large scale. Similarly, of the 1st movements of the last five pianoforte sonatas, four have no coda at all, while that of K.457 is a weighty affair. The ten mature string quartets make a better showing, five of them having significant codas to the 1st movement, though of these, three are very short.

Haydn's case is different; we have seen that his common mature practice is to expand his recapitulations into something more like perorations based upon the material of his expositions. Clearly, such processes will include within themselves all that is needed of winding-up material, and it will be

[34] *Musical Articles from the* Encyclopædia Britannica, page 215.

a waste of time to argue as to how much of the ending shall be regarded as 'coda'. Haydn's earlier works rarely include a coda at all.

Beethoven's early tendency and almost universal practice in maturity, is to add to a recapitulation of Mozartian orthodoxy of outline, a coda which is itself a peroration, often of the proportions of those which so frequently *replace* the recapitulation in Haydn. In other words, the large scale of his designs demands more than either Haydn's or Mozart's normal practice can give. These codas of Beethoven's become, in his second and third creative periods, not only weighty developments of material, but integral parts of the design, with immense artistic significance, often picking up strands left loose by the composer, and indulging in the kind of tonal adventures which are designed by very contrast to emphasise the stability of the home-key.

The coda of the first movement of his 3rd symphony is an excellent example to start with, since it clearly shows the connection between such an extended peroration and the formal cadence emphasis which is its forerunner in so many of Mozart's movements. It thus provides a useful introduction to the much more subtle and elaborate procedure in the gigantic codas of Beethoven's last five symphonies, and those of Brahms. The coda of the finale of Beethoven's 5th symphony is worth particularly careful study for its impassioned treatment of each of the four themes of the movement in turn, though not in their original order; it is a relentless, non-stop piece of writing which, properly played, takes the breath away.

Of the three movements which have served as examples for this chapter, the Mozart has no coda at all; the Haydn has a brief peroration consisting of a restatement of the first theme followed by the closing-theme of the second group, which had been omitted from the recapitulation, played twice and rounded-off with a couple of bars of tonic chord. The Beethoven, also short, follows a frequent practice of this composer, starting the coda in the same manner as the development: that is to say, in this case, with a reversion to the matter and style of the introduction; it is followed by a brief and almost formal statement of the first part of the first group, rounded off with strong cadence-chords. As an illustration of the developing importance of the coda even in Beethoven's early practice, it is excellent; but for examples of the more significant thing that it was to become, the student is referred not only to the symphonic movements mentioned above, but to the 1st movements of the pianoforte sonatas *op. 31 no. 3, op. 53, op. 57,* and *op. 81a.*

Conclusion

The student, if he has attended carefully to the foregoing, and has made it his business to *listen* to the effects described, should not only be able to begin discovering for himself the inner secrets of the music of the classical masters, but should have acquired attentive and methodical habits of listening which will enable him the more easily to understand the music of later composers. We must again issue the warning that, while it may be true that symphonies by Brahms, Dvořák, Tchaikovsky, Elgar, Bruckner, Sibelius and Vaughan Williams are 'in sonata form', they stand or fall as works of art according to the suitability of the design for its content. Many methods of varying or 'improving' the sonata form have been attempted, from Berlioz's mild efforts to achieve unity between movements by transference of themes from one to another, to Liszt's ambitious process of including all his movements in one gigantic 'sonata form.' Insofar as such efforts are the outcome of the demands of the material for scope in special directions, they may prove satisfactory designs, and therefore of artistic value; insofar as they are deliberate and preconceived patterns to which material is made to fit, they will be self-conscious and sterile. No amount of recapitulating the second group before the first 'because the result is more perfectly symmetrical than otherwise' will prove of itself an advance upon Beethoven. As a matter of fact, that particular device was not unknown to Mozart, and like all other such devices, it tends to imply a conception of music in terms of space, rather than of time. It may be a pleasant pastime to form a mental picture of a sonata as if it were a piece of masonry, but to call the image 'musical design' is to deceive oneself.

Many classical slow movements, and occasional scherzi (e.g., Beethoven, op. 31 no. 3) conform to the sonata form skeleton. One need not necessarily expect to find in such slow movements the dramatic elements which go to make the 'sonata style'; for the essence of the slow movement, as a rule, is its lyricism. Hence there may be scope for ornamental variations of recapitulation and other graceful artifices, as in Mozart's 'Jupiter' symphony; or the composer may use the form to parade a seemingly endless stream of gorgeous tunes, as in Beethoven's 2nd symphony. On the other hand, much may be done in a few bars in slow tempo, and some slow movements, such as that in Beethoven's 1st symphony, have short development-sections of an extremely dramatic kind, which serve as an admirable contrast to the lyrical outpourings of the expositions. But observe that such a use of the development section (i.e., as a complete contrast of mood) is in itself opposed to the sonata style, whose essence is continuous dramatic movement to an inevitable end.

VI

VARIANTS OF THE SONATA FORM

1. *The Abridged Sonata form*

THE 'ABRIDGED SONATA FORM', or sonata form without development, is a convenient medium for lyrical movements in which the contrast of keys between the main themes is a matter of relief for the ear rather than of dramatic opposition. It is frequently found in the slow movements of classical sonatas, symphonies and so on, the *adagio* movement of our Mozart K.332 being a perfect example, including decorative variation of the second group upon recapitulation.[35]

Little need be said about this form, whose suitability for slow movements is apparent; some examples, such as that mentioned, proceed without any formality whatsoever from the end of the exposition to the recapitulation. More commonly, perhaps, as in the slow movement of Beethoven's *Pianoforte sonata op. 31 no. 2,* a link of one or more bars is used to make a smooth transition back to the home-tonic.

The 'abridged sonata form', in a peculiarly standardised shape, became the orthodox pattern for the overtures to early nineteenth-century Italian opera. For example, Rossini used it almost (though not quite) exclusively. The formula (for such it is in this case) is well illustrated in his overture to *The Barber of Seville* thus:

Bar 1	Slow introduction, ending formally on the dominant.
Bar 25	First theme, of a bustling nature, in the tonic.

[35] So the autograph. Interestingly enough, however, according to Raymar the early editions printed an apparently authentic variant reading in which the *first* group (but *not* the second) is embellished. The Associated Board edition prints both versions, with Raymar's very valuable notes.

Bar 48	Formal transition, leading to the dominant of the related key.
Bar 92	Second theme, of a gay lyrical nature, in the relative major.
Bar 115	Closing formalities.
Bar 150	Short link leading back to home-dominant. Purely formal and unrelated to subject matter of the exposition.
Bar 154	Recapitulation, modified only to allow the second theme to appear in the tonic major key.
Bar 225	Formal coda, ending with many reinforcements of the final cadence and the final tonic chord.

Examples for analysis:

Rossini	Overtures to *Semiramide, The Thieving Magpie, The Italian in Algiers, The Silken Ladder,* etc.
Boieldieu	Overture to *La Dame Blanche.*
Mozart	Overture to *The Marriage of Figaro.*
	Symphony no. 34 (slow movement)
	String Quartet (K.387) (slow movement).
Beethoven	*Pianoforte sonata (op. 2 no. 1)* (slow movement)
	Pianoforte sonata (op. 10 no. 1) (slow movement)
	Pianoforte sonata (op. 31 no. 2) (slow movement)

2. *The Sonata-Rondo*

The sonata-rondo is a hybrid form containing elements of both sonata form and the simple rondo, and claims special attention as being the favourite design for the final movements of classical concertos. It is also frequently found doing the same duty in sonatas, more rarely in works for the larger chamber-music combinations, and very seldom in symphonies.[36]

It differs from the sonata-form, anatomically speaking, in that the themes tend to be well-defined melodies rather than organised groups of material; that the first theme or group is restated in the tonic key immediately after the second has been given out; and that the development tends normally to

[36] The finale of Beethoven's *6th symphony,* however, is in sonata-rondo form, though this fact has been missed by at least one so-called authority.

be episodical; that is to say, it may be an episode in a related key: or it may be partly episode, partly development; though plenty of cases exist where it is pure development, tending, however, to stick more closely to one key-centre than is the case in the sonata form.

Looked at from a different angle, it is seen to differ from the simple rondo form in that the first episode is recapitulated in the tonic key after the second return of the main theme.

The skeleton may be drawn thus:

'A1' Main theme in tonic.
Transition leading to threshold of related key.
'B1' Second theme in related key.
'A2' First return of main theme in tonic.
'C' Episode and/or development, centred in a related key, or in the tonic minor.
'A3' Second return of main theme in tonic.
Transition modified to remain in tonic.
'B2' Return of second theme in tonic.
'A4' Final return of main theme in tonic, usually amalgamated with coda which, however, is sometimes independent of it.

It will be apparent that such a scheme is more concerned with the quality of its material than with its dramatic possibilities—in other words, the type of material which will lend itself to this kind of design is likely to show its best qualities at once, rather than to wait for the subtleties of development to bring their latent significance to the surface. Hence, sonata-rondos in general (like other rondos) are less exacting in their demands upon the listener's attention, tending to give pleasure with relatively little effort of concentration.

Upon rare occasions the form has been used (as, it was earlier observed, has the simple rondo form) for slow movements of great beauty and depth; the classic example is the slow movement of Beethoven's 4th symphony.

The example which we have chosen is characteristic of its kind. Study of the movements in the list which follows its analysis will reveal many variants of detail born of the nature of the material and the genius of the composer.

Beethoven—Pianoforte sonata in C minor, op. 13, last movt.

'A1'	1-17	First theme in C minor. An 8-bar sentence, its second phrase repeated and the whole rounded off with a 5-bar phrase reaching a strong full-close.
Trans.	18-25	In two sequential steps through F minor to the dominant of E flat. Closing into:
'B1'	25-61	First episode (or second subject) in the relative major, in two parts (25-43 and 44-61), swinging over at the end to finish on the dominant of the home-key.
'A2'	62-78	First return of main theme, exactiy as bars 1-17.
'C'	79-120	Second episode (or middle section) based on the related key of A flat major. 79-107 is a little self-contained 'open 3-part form' with its first 8-bar part repeated, interrupted at its end to lead to the dominant of C. Bars 107-120 consist of preparation on this dominant, with a gradual crescendo leading to a pause.
'A3'	121-128	The main 8-bar sentence of the first theme only.
Trans.	129-134	The main theme, instead of continuing as in 'A1' and 'A2', develops its chief figure into a short new transition passing through F minor and ending on the home-dominant.
'B2'	135-170	Second theme in tonic major key. The first part is somewhat modified; the second, after giving out its first phrase, proceeds to a short passage of self-development ending on the dominant.
'A4'	171-182	The first 12 bars of the original main theme, melodically embellished as to the repetition of the second phrase.
Coda	183-210	Based upon material found in 'A' and 'B'.

The following are suitable further examples for analysis and study:

Beethoven	The last movements of the following pianoforte sonatas:
	op. 2 no. 2; op. 26; op. 28; op. 31 no. 1.
	op. 14 no. 1, a special case with return of the first episode in the subdominant.
	op. 27 no. 1 and op. 90, in each of which the 2nd episode consists entirely of development.
	Rondo in G (op. 51 no. 2).
	Finales of pianoforte concertos *nos. 1, 2* and *3.*

Brahms	Finales of the pianoforte concertos in *D minor* and *B flat.*
Mozart	Finales of the pianoforte sonatas *K.310, 311* and *333.*

The above discussion and examples, while they cover most of the ground, by no means exhaust the possibilities which the great composers have found in the rondo principle. Mozart, for example, in several of his concertos [e.g., the well-known D minor (K. 466) and A major (K.488) for pianoforte], writes rondo-finales showing special individual features. An attempt to classify these would take up more space than we could afford, and would probably end up with as many categories as there are movements; in any case, it would serve little purpose, since anybody who has followed this chapter will recognise such features for himself. Likewise, on a smaller scale, rondos are found which do not conform to the convenient standards of design laid down by some theorists. Such, for instance, are the slow movements of Mozart's piano sonata K.311 and Beethoven's op. 2 no. 3, and the finale of the latter's op. 49 no. 1. Each of these movements, with varying degrees of internal organisation, is built on the plan A-B-A-B-A, in which 'B' recurs in a key different from that in which it was first heard. Again, Mozart's rondo in D (K.485) is clearly a sonata form of the monothematic type usually associated with Haydn; presumably it owes its name to the extremely numerous recurrences of the chief theme in many different keys. Finally, attention is drawn to the structurally unique finale of Mozart's last pianoforte sonata (K.576). Theorists with a passion for tidiness have wrangled for generations over this movement,[37] which clearly shows the main features of a rondo, viz., several recurrences of the main theme in the tonic key. Equally clearly, a second section in the dominant is recapitulated in the tonic, and a middle section (occurring immediately after the first restatement of the first theme), dis-

[37] Aubyn Raymar and R. O. Morris are honourable exceptions.

cursive as to key, is easily definable. The trouble is that all the sections are built out of the same thematic material. Luckily for us, Mozart's genius for doing the right thing in the right place transcends all passions for pigeon-holing, and the result is a movement of great beauty and formal strength.

VII

THE CONCERTO

THE BASIC PROBLEM to be solved by the composer who writes a concerto is the same as that with which he is faced when writing for a solo singer with orchestral accompaniment—i.e., how to make the best use of the more-or-less elaborate and expensive forces which will be at his command; for, as Tovey has pointed out, it would be absurd and wasteful to gather together so many musicians unless all are employed for a positive artistic purpose; while, on the other hand, there is the difficulty that the orchestral forces, by sheer force of numbers and volume of sound, will tend to swamp the solo unless they are kept in a subordinate position.

In essentials, these factors have remained unchanged from the seventeenth century to the present day, that is, since the orchestra came into being; and the handling of them by composers within the general framework of the style of the various periods in which they lived and worked, has governed the whole structure of the concerto forms.

The earliest composers to work out a completely satisfactory solution were the writers of seventeenth-century opera, of whom Alessandro Scarlatti is the most renowned. His method, which was followed by Handel and Bach in the hundreds of solo arias and duets (and many of the choruses) in their sacred and secular works, employed the orchestra in such a way as to give it scope to develop its own personality, as well as to act as accompanist and partner to the soloist, and it led naturally to the standardisation of a formal skeleton which, for reasons which will appear in a moment, is known as the *ritornello* form. Any fruitful discussion of the evolution of the concerto must proceed by stages beginning with an examination of this form; the present chapter is divided into four parts, as follows:

1. The ritornello form.
2. The concerto up to the time of Bach.
3. The classical concerto of Mozart, Beethoven and Brahms.
4. The post-classical concerto.

1. *The ritornello form*

This form presents us with a skeleton capable of supporting an infinity of varied designs; it is that used normally in the first or main section of the crude 3-part form known as the *da capo* form (see page 40). It must be clearly understood that it is the internal organisation of this particular section that is under review, and not the *da capo* aria as a whole. As a matter of fact, many of the arias and choruses in the works of Bach and Handel are complete within the limits of the *ritornello* form, and do not have a middle section or *da capo* at all.

The name is derived from the *ritornello* or instrumental introduction which opens the proceedings, and which 'returns' at intervals between the musical paragraphs which make up the solo part. Briefly, the procedure is as follows: the *ritornello,* a substantial musical section, complete in itself, and containing some or all of the main features of the piece, is played by the orchestra; it is well-grounded in the tonic key, in which it finishes with a strong full-close, and any modulations which may take place during its course are of the most transitory and incidental kind. At the close of the *ritornello,* the soloist, opening in the tonic key, delivers a musical paragraph which may be in part or whole based upon thematic material contained in the *ritornello,* or may be entirely new. This first solo paragraph modulates to a related key, usually the dominant or the relative major, in which it in turn makes a full close. The *ritornello* re-enters *in this new key*, usually in a substantially shortened version; and the form is worked out at greater or less length by a continuation of this process of solo paragraphs closing into a variety of related keys, punctuated by parts of the *ritornello* (or sometimes the whole of it) given in the said keys, and in their turn modulating to new keys. The process is wound up by a final statement of the complete *ritornello* in the tonic key, the soloist having brought his last paragraph to a full close there.

It is worth remarking that many arias show the form at its smallest possible, with only one middle statement of the *ritornello* between two solo paragraphs, the first of which moves to the dominant, and the second back (perhaps by devious ways) to the tonic; in essentials, however, such an aria is no different from some of the huge ritornello forms, covering the whole range of key-relations, to be found in the works of Bach.

First, let us examine an easily accessible ritornello form on a small scale:

Bach—Cradle-song ('Slumber, beloved') from the *Christmas Oratorio.*

Bars 1-28 Ritornello-theme in the key of G major. It includes three distinct parts, each built on a separate idea, viz., 1-8, 9-16, and 16-28. Though touching various related keys, it is quite firmly in the tonic, ending there with a full close.

Bars 29-56 First solo paragraph, starting in the tonic and closing firmly in the dominant key. (Observe in passing that the voice is doubled throughout by a solo flute playing an octave higher; this helps to clarify the vocal line, and to distinguish it from the accompanying texture, which is built up out of figures from the first and second parts of the ritornello-theme.)

Bars 57-68 Ritornello-theme in the dominant key. It is shortened, only the third part being given; in other words, this is substantially a transposition of bars 16-28.

Bars 69-96 Second solo-paragraph, starting in the dominant and closing in the tonic.

Bars 97-112 Final appearance of the *ritornello* in the tonic key, consisting of the first and second parts only, with a full close.

Note that this part is followed by a middle-section in E minor, with the customary formality of the *'da capo'* indication, showing that a complete restatement of the main section described above is to follow it. Notwithstanding that it makes some slight use of the third idea from the ritornello-theme, the middle section is entirely independent.

Well-known examples of small-scale ritornello forms are Handel's 'O had I Jubal's Lyre', 'How beautiful are the feet' and 'Thou shalt break them'. The first is from the oratorio *Joshua,* the other two from *Messiah.*

For our next example, we go to Bach's secular cantata (no. 211) 'Schweigt stille, plaudert nicht', usually known as the *Coffee Cantata,* and the student is earnestly recommended to provide himself with a copy of this easily accessible work, which contains several excellent examples of ritornello arias. The first 'Hat man nicht mit seinen Kindern', illustrates well a more elaborate use of the form than those cited above, albeit no longer than most of them:

Bars 1-7 Ritornello-theme. It divides into two parts, 1-3 and 4-7, coming to a full close in the tonic, D major.

Bars 7-17 First solo, starting in the tonic and closing in the dominant. It illustrates a feature so common in such arias as to be almost 'normal', namely, a false start whereby the soloist gives out one sentence only, is interrupted by a bar or two of the *ritornello,* and makes a fresh start identical with the first, but this time continuing to complete the paragraph.

Bars 17-21 The second part of the *ritornello* only, in the dominant.

Bars 21-30 Second solo, from A major via F sharp minor, E minor and A minor to a full close in the subdominant, G major.

Bars 30-32 Third appearance of the *ritornello, first* part only.

Bars 32-42 Third solo, from G major through B minor to a full close in F sharp minor.

Bars 42-44 Second part of *ritornello* shortened. F sharp minor to the home dominant.

Bars 44-63 Recapitulatory section consisting of (i) the complete *ritornello* in the tonic key (44-50), with the solo singing during its first part; (ii) a final solo in the tonic key (50-57); and (iii) the complete *ritornello,* exactly as at the start.

Of the other ritornello forms in the *Coffee Cantata,* no. 4 ('Ei! wie schmeckt der Coffee!') is not dissimilar in scope to the one just discussed, but illustrates another feature, viz., the employment of a solo instrument (in this case a flute) for the purpose of giving a distinctive colour to the whole piece. The solo instrument takes the lead in the *ritornello,* and during the vocal sections intertwines itself with the singer's melodic line. (Bach frequently employs a solo instrument in this way, determining his choice of instrument and fashioning its melodic line with a view to underlining the prevailing mood of the words, or illustrating almost pictorially some prominent feature contained in the text.) No. 6 ('Mädchen, die von harten Sinnen') is again similar in general outline, while no. 8 ('Heute noch') provides another example of the 'false start', and has a minor middle section (based upon similar material to the main part) and formal *da capo.* The finale ('Die Katze lässt das Mausen nicht') is a vocal trio in ritornello form of a very simple kind, with the unusual feature of *two* alternating middle sections with *da capo* after each; an extension of the crude 3-part aria form to a crude simple-rondo form.

One word more, and enough will have been said on this subject to enable the student to understand the construction of any ritornello form he is likely to meet; composers, and particularly Bach, used the form as the basis of enormous choral movements of which the texture and method of writing are strictly fugal (see chapter ix). Such movements are often described as fugues, with an implication that no more need be said as to the general basis of their construction. A pure fugue, however, such as 'Gratias agimus tibi' from Bach's *Mass in B minor,* is entirely different from the ritornello-chorus (which may be partly or mostly *in* fugue) such as the gigantic 'Kyrie eleison' from the same work.

In this movement, after a four-bar introduction, we find an orchestral ritornello of 25 bars, leading into a choral section (in fugue) of 43 bars, ending in the dominant. short intervention of part of the *ritornello* (8 bars) leads back to the tonic, where the second great choral section opens. It lasts for 46 bars, to the end of the piece.

Now, this seems on the face of it to have little to do with the forms we have been considering, until we examine the choral parts more closely, when we discover that bars 48-72 and 102-126 are complete statements of the *ritornello* in the dominant and tonic respectively. In other words, this massive piece of musical architecture is a ritornello form in which the chorus represents the solo part, and at the same time takes its full share in the *ritornelli* themselves. So soon as this fundamental fact has been grasped, the details of the fugal construction, the subtleties of the key-relationships between one section and another, and the balance of the sections themselves, take on a new meaning, and the perfect proportions of the giant movement are fully revealed.[38]

For further study, the following examples, all taken from Bach's *Mass in B minor,* are recommended. In brackets are given the names of the instruments carrying the main burden of the *ritornello,* and giving a characteristic colour to the whole movement.

No. 2	Christe eleison (all the violins in unison).
No. 5	Laudamus te (solo violin).
No. 9	Qui sedes ad dextram patris (Oboe d'amore).
No. 10	Quoniam (Horn and bassoons).
No. 14	Et in unum dominum (2 oboi d'amore).
No. 18	Et in spiritum sanctum (2 oboi d'amore).

(2) The Concerto up to the time of J. S. Bach.

The development of instrumental technique, especially of the violin family, during the seventeenth century, encouraged a tendency which showed itself very early in the history of instrumental music, that of contrasting a small group of highly-skilled solo players with the larger group which was the main body of the orchestra. The leading members of the various string families, who were naturally as a rule the best players, were thus combined into a small 'concertino' in contrast to the 'concerto grosso' with whom they played

[38] Bach used the ritornello form also for extended instrumental movements. E.g., the Prelude to the *3rd English Suite.*

now together, now in alternating antiphonal effects, now in more-or-less elaborate decorative passages with fairly simple accompaniment.

Relying at first upon successions of the small forms of which the chamber- and church-sonatas of the period were formed, composers gradually, by experiment and experience, evolved a 'concerto style' showing vigorous rhythmic characteristics and a clear differentiation between *solo and tutti*; the development of the style may be seen in the works of Stradella and Corelli, and its perfection in the *Concerti Grossi* of Handel. The problems involved were very similar to those in the aria, and it became more and more apparent that their solution lay along similar lines—viz., in forms based upon a recurrent orchestral *ritornello*. In the hands of Vivaldi, who extended the concerto grosso idea to concertos written for all kinds of groups of solo instruments, wind, string or mixtures of the two, the forms became more clearly defined, reaching perfection in J. S. Bach's six *Brandenburg concertos*, which are concerti grossi on the biggest scale, with a different group of solo instruments in each. The importance and high organisation of the main movement, supplemented by the influence of other instrumental forms which were being developed simultaneously, rendered it no longer necessary or desirable to have large numbers of little movements in a concerto, and the three-movement idea, in the order quick-slow-quick became the natural and accepted sequence. Of these, the first was the chief in importance, length, and subtlety of design, and is the main concern of this part of the chapter. The slow movements were of various kinds; often broad cantilena movements in open 2-part form, with rich harmonic accompaniment; or ostinato basses, or slow dance-movements. The finales were usually quick fugal movements, dances or ritornello forms on a rather smaller and lighter scale than the impressive opening movements.

The movement which is analysed below is an example of the concerto grosso first movement at its highest stage of development.

It employs a 'concertino' of four solo instruments (trumpet, flute, oboe and violin) in conjunction with an orchestra of strings, and illustrates to perfection Bach's handling of the problem of doing justice to everybody. The similarity between this design and that of the arias analysed above is so apparent as to need no stressing; it is here more immediately obvious than in certain other works (e.g. the *Brandenburg concertos nos. 3* and *6*), where the score does not so clearly define which are *solo-* and which *tutti-sections,* but in which (provided they are well played) the ear can grasp the essential contrasts of style quite clearly.

Bach—Brandenburg concerto no. 2, 1st movement.

The movement opens with the following 8-bar ritornello-theme, given out by the full forces; the trumpet having a simplified line of its own, the other soloists playing in unison with the orchestral first violins:

Ex. 11

Examination shows that this ritornello-theme recurs at intervals in various keys, reaching a strong full-close in each, and the movement is most conveniently divided into sections concluding with these punctuation-marks.

1. Bars 1-8 — *Ritornello,* key F major, containing the figures a, a′, b, b′, c, c′, d, e, e′ and f, in which a′, b′, c′ and e′ are sub-figures contained within larger figures. All these figures are developed independently in the sequel.

2. Bars 9-28 — The four solo-instruments are introduced one at a time with a new 'solo theme'; their entries are separated by tutti statements of the first 2 bars of the ritornello-theme. After the second solo-entry, the music swings over to the dominant key, in which the remainder of the section is given. (Compare this with the 'false start' of the typical mature ritornello-aria.) After the last solo entry, bars 3-8 of the ritornello-theme (i.e. that part of it which had not been used for the interventions *between* the solo entries) are given by the tutti, coming to a full close in the dominant key of C major.

3. Bars 29-39 — Up to bar 35 we have a solo-section, led by the trumpet giving the 'solo theme' in the tonic. The music moves to the key of D minor, and to material from the *ritornello,* through a broad sequence featuring figure c′ in the bass. At bar 36 the tutti takes over the main business, giving the latter half of the *ritornello,* and closing strongly in D minor.

4. Bars 40-59 — This section falls into three parts: (i) from 40 to 49 figs. a, b, b inverted and e receive broad sequential treatment, the soloists being lightly accompanied by the tutti. The harmony, leaving D minor, is unstable, being a series of dominants running into one another. (ii) From 50-55 the texture is thinned-out, and the harmony shifts slowly through a series of chords of the 7th to the dominant of B flat. (iii) From 56-59 the second part of the ritornello-theme is given in B flat by the tutti, the chief melodic line being in the bass at 56-57. There is a strong full-close in B flat at bar 59.

5. Bars 60-83 — 60-67 is a section of pure solo-work with continuo accompaniment only. The four solo-instruments are brought in one by one with the 'solo theme', in a transparent counterpoint which reaches five parts at bar 66. They start in B flat, passing through G minor and E flat to C

minor. At 68 the main force enters the discussion with material from the ritornello-theme in C minor. From 72-74 the orchestra is relegated to the role of accompanist, and the harmony shifts over to G minor. 75-83 is substantially a transposition of 31-39, the ritornello-theme entering here at bar 80 with a full close in G minor at 83, corresponding to that in D minor at bar 39.

6. Bars 84-102 Soli and bass discuss several ritornello-figures for 16 bars. The upper orchestral strings maintain a steady harmonic filling-up with occasional moments of thematic importance, while the music passes through D minor and A minor. From 94-99 activity increases (these bars being in effect a transposition of 31-35) and lead to a full tutti entry of the second half of the ritornello-theme in A minor at 99. Its full-close at 103 comes to a full stop on the unison A, whereupon the next section begins at once in F major.

7. Bars 103-118 Final section in the home-key. The whole ritornello is given as at the beginning, except that the first two bars are in full unison. It is, however, divided into two 4-bar parts, between which (bars 107-114) comes a last solo-section with purely harmonic orchestral support. This is a modified and slightly extended transposition of the section at bars 50-54; and as that section led to the last 4 bars of the *ritornello* in B flat, so does this lead to the ultimate tonic statement of the completion of the ritornello-theme which was begun at 103-106.

The form of this movement as a whole (and of many others constructed on similar lines) reminds one, as Tovey points out in another connection,[39] of a solid piece of architecture buttressed round on all sides. The buttresses are the recurrent tuttis (in this case one and one only in each of the 5 keys which are closely related to the tonic) with their solid full-closes, and the main supports are the massive tonic entries at the start and finish.

[39] *Essays in Musical Analysis,* vol. II, p. 183.

The following movements from concerti grossi will repay study and analysis. (First movement in every case):

Vivaldi	Almost any one of the innumerable concertos with a group of solo-instruments.
J. S. Bach	*Brandenburg concertos nos. 1, 3, 5, 6.* *Concerto in D minor for 2 violins and strings.* *Concerto in A minor for flute, violin, harpsichord and strings.*

The highest stage of concerto-organisation reached during the period under discussion is found in those concertos of Bach which have a single solo-instrument.

The credit for being the first composer to take the logical step of writing music which transfers the *rôle* of concertino to a single player of considerable technical skill is variously ascribed to Albinoni and Torelli; in any case, the step was taken about the year 1700. Here again, Vivaldi is the link between the earlier composers and Bach, whose small number of examples includes the finest things of the kind in existence. While the basic conception of contrast between solo and tutti forces remains fundamental in the solo concerto, the rivalry between solo and tutti becomes more acute, insofar as the contrast is greater. In other words, where the *concertino* of a concerto grosso is employed chiefly to provide antiphonal effects with the tutti, and to afford relief and contrast to it, the single solo part of a solo concerto is bound to develop its own special characteristics as an individual, and hence to a greater or less extent to include the display of virtuosity as one of its methods of expression. As will be seen, the great composers have always made this aspect subservient to the claims of the whole *as music,* whereas lesser men, especially those who were themselves virtuoso players, have written so-called concertos as a means of providing opportunities for the display of technical fireworks and little else.

We may expect, then, to find the chief movements of Bach's solo concertos following the same general lines as his concerti grossi, but with the solo parts developed at greater length and requiring greater skill for their execution. The example we have chosen for close analysis is the first movement of his largest and greatest solo concerto. It will be observed that besides the 'buttressing' by the *ritornello* with its full-closes in various related keys, there are considerable stretches of transposed recapitulation which give strength and great stability to the structure.

Bach—Concerto in D minor for clavier and strings (1st movement).

This concerto, which is found among Bach's works in more than one form, is certainly an arrangement or adaptation of a lost earlier original in which a violin was the solo instrument. This fact is clear from the nature of much of the writing in the solo-part. Many movements and complete works among Bach's instrumental compositions are transcriptions of this kind.

Bars 1-7	Ritornello-theme containing the figures a, a′, a″, b, c, d, all detachable and subsequently used and developed. The theme is given out in full unison.

Ex. 12

Bars 7-12	New solo-theme in the tonic key, lightly accompanied by the tutti.

Bars 13-22 — Tutti statement of ritornello-theme in tonic, now in imitative counterpoint, extended after 5 bars to lead to a full-close in the dominant key. Closing into:

Bars 22-56 — Solo theme in the dominant, accompanied as before. At bar 28, the orchestra begins to develop figs. a and b in imitation between 1st and 2nd violins, accompanied by broken-chord figuration from the solo. The music passes in broad sequences through several related keys to reach a strong full-close in F major at bar 40; thence to bar 46 the soloist discusses figs. a, b and a′, reaching a half-close in A minor which proves in the sequel to be of significance. Thereafter the violins develop fig. c in very close imitation with running accompaniment on the keyboard, closing into the next section at bar 56.

Bars 56-62 — Full dominant statement of ritornello-theme by the tutti, harmonised in imitative counterpoint as at bar 13. Closing into:

Bars 62-104 — New (second) solo-theme, obviously of violin origin, with harmonic filling-up by orchestral violins. It is given out first in A minor; a moduating bar (69) leads to E minor, in which key the whole theme is re-stated. The solo continuing the figuration which now becomes purely harmonic in its significance, the violins combine in close dialogue for two bars on fig. c, giving way to the violas at bar 79, who provide the bass for the next 12 bars. At 82 the figuration of the solo changes, but the music remains harmonic in feeling. The viola-bass reaches the dominant of C and over a 6-bar dominant-pedal the harmony gradually settles down, moving definitely into C major at bar 91. There the solo introduces figs. a and b momentarily, and in a florid passage accompanied by the orchestra, works up to a full-close in G minor at bar 104. This section closes into:

Bars 104-113 — Complete ritornello-theme stated by tutti in the sub-dominant (G minor), harmonised with imitative counterpoint quite different in detail from that at bars 13 or 56. It comes upon a strongly discordant interruption just before its normal ending. After a 3-bar cadenza in rushing demi-semiquavers, the full-close is completed by solo and orchestra. Closing into:

Bars 113-134 Figs. a and b developed by solo and orchestra. starting in G minor, to D minor at bar 116, and so to bars 122-134 which recapitulate 28-40 a fourth higher. We thus finish this section in B flat major, which is at once treated as the dominant of E flat.

Bars 134-172 The solo has accompanied passage-work modulating quickly through several keys in a short time. From 148 the material of the 'second solo' is developed over a tonic pedal D, the orchestra being silent after 153. Thence in a generalised harmonic passage to 162, where the bass changes, the orchestra re-enters with light harmonic support, and the piano adopts a new figuration. The bass rises by steps to B flat, and thereafter sags gently by semitones, over a pedal A to 168. This purely harmonic cadenza-like passage finally reaches the home-dominant chord at bar 171.

Bars 172-190 The tutti burst in with the ritornello-theme in the home-key, in unison; but after two bars the solo intervenes, with the orchestra taking over the accompaniment in imitative treatment of fig. c, as at bar 46. In fact, 174 to the end is a transposition, now in the tonic key, of 46-62. As the latter passage ended in a dominant-key full-close, so now does it end in a tonic close, completing the whole design; that is, the final statement of the *ritornello* in the tonic from 184-190 corresponds to the dominant statement in the middle of the movement at 56-62. The final statement, however, for greater impressiveness, is in unison as at the opening.

The student who has followed the above analysis closely will be well advised next to give his attention to the last movement of the same work which, rather exceptionally, is on a scale and of a scope little smaller than the first movement. He should make a detailed analysis on similar lines to the above. Close study of these two movements with the score, coupled to attentive listening in the light of the theoretical knowledge thus gained, will do more to promote understanding of the principles involved than any text-book can do.

The concerto of the Bach period is neglected to a surprising extent by writers on musical structure, which may in part account for the widespread misunderstanding of the classical concerto which is the subject of the next section of this chapter, and for the nonsense which has been written about it.

The following movements of concertos by Bach will likewise repay study:

Clavier concerto in E (1st and 3rd movements).

Violin concerto in E (1st and 3rd movements) (or *Clavier concerto in D,* which is a transcription of the same work.)

The above are in full aria-form with middle section and *da capo;* their structure is much simpler than that of the D minor.

Clavier concerto in F minor (1st and 3rd movements).

Violin concerto in A minor (1st movement) (or *Clavier concerto in G minor,* which is the same work in another form.)

'Italian' Concerto for harpsichord (1st and 3rd movements.)[40]

(3) The classical concerto of Mozart, Beethoven and Brahms.

There is a widespread belief that the Mozartian concerto-form is ' "simply" a sonata for soloist with orchestra' in the same way that a symphony is a 'sonata for full orchestra'. This is a dangerous half-truth based upon a very superficial examination of the facts; to accept it without reserve is to ignore the special conditions set up by the opposition of the individual and the mass, which are fundamental. These conditions, which were met in the days of Bach's 'architectural' structures by forms based upon the underlying *ritornello* idea, gave rise, in the period of 'dramatic' forms to certain features

[40] This work was written for a big 2-manual harpsichord on which, by alternation of manuals and coupling of the octave above and below by mechanical means, it was possible to differentiate between 'solo' and 'tutti' effects. Yet one of the best-known of textbooks of musical form describes it as 'for clavichord (*sic*) and more like a solo-sonata'. (!)

which are found only in the concertos of Mozart, Beethoven and Brahms (with perhaps one or two other isolated cases), and which the theorist who believes in the 'sonata for soloist and orchestra' idea must explain away as best he can, if he does not ignore them altogether or dismiss them as anachronisms.[41]

It is, of course, true that the conditions which brought about the change from the essentially rhetorical forms of Bach to the essentially dramatic ones of Mozart wrought a revolution in the concerto also; but these conditions did not and could not alter the basic physical relationship between solo and tutti in which common sense and artistic economy equally require that soloist and orchestra should each play their full part, the latter neither swamping the former, nor effacing itself by becoming a mere harmonic support. Thus it comes about that the classical concertos display a unique feature, unknown to any other form, in the processional array of themes which precede the main entry of the soloist; an array designed to allow the orchestra to set forth some of the main material of the movement without entering into the realms of dramatic action, controversy or discussion; and at the same time, to arouse anticipation of the more colourful and active events which will follow the entry of the solo part, itself the first dramatic stroke. This opening tutti is clearly allied to and derived from the Bach-type *ritornello*, in that it gives the gist of the movement, without committing itself to decisive action of the kind which is fundamental to a symphonic exposition; it is here above all that misunderstandings have arisen, and on this topic that so much nonsense has been written by people who apparently look at music but do not listen to it. All talk of 'double expositions' and of 'equivalents to repeated expositions' should be

[41] It is disconcerting and disappointing in these post-Tovey days to find an article in a Pelican publication entitled *Music 1950*, issued under the editorship of so good a musician as Ralph Hill (but not written by him) subscribing to these antiquated heresies, and actually propagating them.

regarded as suspect, since scarcely one of the two-score-and-odd classical concertos which exist will lend it support. The difference between the opening tutti of a concerto and its real exposition is like that between a procession and an act of a play.

The scheme of the classical concerto, then, may be summarised thus:

1. Tutti, akin to a *ritornello,* centred firmly throughout in the tonic, modulations being a purely incidental matter of colour, and undramatic in intention and in effect. This tutti will contain some or all of the themes which will form the subject-matter of the exposition.[42]

2. Entry of the solo, and exposition of the material on sonata lines. The orchestra here tends to accompany rather than to assert itself or to take part in antiphonal give-and-take with the soloist, except that it will usually wind up the exposition by a full *forte* statement of the last part of the tutti, somewhat in the manner of the closing section of a sonata-exposition. Observe that this tutti, being now of course in a complementary key, has much the effect of a middle entry of the *ritornello* in a Bach concerto. Of the exposition it is necessary to say that it may, and usually does, contain one or more themes, usually very prominent ones, which were not heard in the tutti at all; also that it is by no means bound to include all the themes that *were* heard in the tutti, nor to give out those that it does use in the same order in which they appeared in the tutti. These are facts so inconvenient to the school of theorists who regard the tutti as a superfluous survival that they usually ignore them, or gloss over them.

[42] Examples in which the soloist appears at the very beginning of the work, do not affect the main consideration outlined above; for they fall into one of two classes: either they are taking part in an introductory flourish before the tutti begins (as in Beethoven's *5th piano concerto*); or the characteristic quality of the solo instrument is being exploited as a pure effect of colour-contrast (as in Beethoven's *4th piano concerto*). In such cases the soloist soon drops out, leaving the orchestra to the tutti, and to the working-up of excitement for the dramatic event which is the soloist's initiation of the exposition.

3. Development, on the lines of a sonata movement.

4. Recapitulation, which will not be a return of the exposition only, but will reconcile the exposition and the tutti, including material which was common to both, but also that which appeared only in one or the other; except that one or two items of thematic material may be left over for treatment in the coda.

5. A *cadenza* (originally extempore) in which the soloist, entirely alone (bar one or two exceptional and famous instances)[43] may select certain of the themes for treatment appropriate to the characteristics of his instrument.

6. A coda.

All this is very well in its way; the trouble is, that, like all anatomical descriptions, it conveys nothing of the individual life which every great concerto possesses, and which makes it unique. In no sphere of music is it more true to say that every individual is different from every other. Here we propose to analyse one great example, whereby the student may see for himself how the music grows inevitably, giving flesh and blood and indeed soul, to the skeleton which represents the lowest common denominator of all concertos. Thereafter the student must make his own way, examining, with a mind unbiassed by any preconceptions, the music as it is. A fairly comprehensive list is given of those concertos whose first movements will more than reward his trouble. It will be observed that a majority are by Mozart.

Mozart—1st movement of Pianoforte concerto in D minor, K.466.

Tutti:

An array of themes which it will be convenient to identify by numbers, as follows:

(1) bars	1-16	key D minor. Closing into:
(2) bars	16-32	starting as an intensified development of the main feature of (1), but moving on to other features, and ending with formalities leading to a half-close.

[43] The finales of Elgar's and Brahms's *Violin Concertos.*

(3) bars 33-43 A quiet theme starting in F major, but at once proceeding sequentially through G minor and A minor back to D minor.

(4) bars 44-71 A group of ideas capable of considerable subdivision, and for present purposes conveniently classified thus:
- (i) bars 44-48 leading to
- (ii) bars 48-58.
- (i) again. Bars 58-61, leading this time to
- (iii) bars 61-71.

Key D minor throughout.

(5) bars 72-77 D minor.

Note that it is impossible to forecast the likely distribution of these themes in the exposition. At the most we might regard (3) as the probable beginning of the second group, a prognostication which is belied by the event.

Exposition:

Bars 77-114 First group, in two parts:
- (i) bars 77-91. An entirely new theme in the tonic key, given out by the solo unaccompanied until its last four bars. Closing into
- (ii) bars 91-114, theme (1) of the tutti in the orchestra, with running accompaniment from the solo, expanded and rounded off with formalities taken from the close of theme (2), ending with a half-close as in the tutti.

Bars 115-127 Transition. Theme (3) of the tutti treated in dialogue between solo and parts of the orchestra. Extended and modified at its end to lead to the threshold of F major.[44]

Bars 128-192 Second group in F major, in no fewer than five parts:
- (i) bars 128-143. An entirely new theme of 8 bars, given out first by the solo with string accessories, and repeated by the woodwind with solo accessories. Closing into:
- (ii) bars 143-153. New material of a non-lyrical virtuoso type, in which the solo is lightly supported by the strings. Closing into:

[44] Not to the key of C major. *Cf.* p. 71.

(iii) bars 153-174. Part (i) of tutti theme no. 4, expanded as a continuation of the passage-work of the previous section, and leading to new cadential formalities. Closing into:

(iv) bars 174-186. The orchestra alone gives tutti theme no. (2), now in the major, and omitting its cadence-formalities.

(v) bars 187-192. Tutti theme (5), exactly transposed to the relative major, on the orchestra alone.

N.B. Observe that sections (iv) and (v) of the second group fulfil the functions of the *ritornello,* as described on page 109 above.

Development:

Bars 192-254 A spacious single modulating process. The opening strain of the first solo theme is given in the key of F, and leads by way of a 3-bar cascade to a clear-cut modulation based upon the main figure of theme no. (1). Thus reaching G minor, the whole proceeding is repeated with delightful changes of minor detail, the modulation taking us to E flat. Here we have yet a third statement, which this time leads to a longish passage of glittering keyboard figuration. Into this, at regular 4-bar intervals, break the strings with the figure from theme (1), rising one step each time, and thus taking us through F minor, G minor and on to the chord of A which, of course, is the home dominant. Thence (from bar 242) the remainder is dominant preparation for the recapitulation, which appears at bar 254, ushered in by a strikingly dramatic chromatic scale in the solo part.

Recapitulation:

Bars 254-287 First group. Themes (1) and (2) of the tutti, now shared between solo and tutti; the former provides chiefly decorative additions.

Observe that the first solo theme, which bore the main burden of the development section, is absent, and that theme (2) is restored to its important place as an adjunct of the main theme, as in the tutti.

Bars 288-302 Transition. Tutti theme (3) as used in the exposition, and now modified to end on the home-dominant.

Bars 303-365 Second group, now in tonic minor (a change of mode):

(i) bars 303-318. Almost exactly as in the exposition.

(ii) bars 318-330. Passage work similar to, but quite different in detail from, the corresponding section in the exposition. Closing into:

(iii) bars 330-356. The equivalent to section (iii) of the second group of the exposition. Closing into:

(iv) bars 356-365. A curtailed version of the similar exposition passage, derived from theme (2) of the tutti. It ends on a 6/4 chord, with pause for the cadenza.

Observe that the final section (v) of the second group, which closed both tutti and exposition, is absent from the recapitulation. The reason will be apparent in a moment.

Cadenza:

Coda:

Bars 366-397 Up to bar 390 this consists of the whole of tutti themes (4) and (5) exactly as at the end of the tutti, except for some shortening of repetitive passages. Apart from its main feature, theme (4) has never been heard since then; while theme (5) is that one which was left over from the recapitulation, and thus appears here with all the more force. At the point (bar 390) which corresponds to the original first entry of the solo, the coda moves into a short concluding passage of cadential formalities based upon the opening theme of the concerto.

The coda, it will be seen, has many of the outward signs, as well as all the meaning, of the final *ritornello* of a Bach concerto; and indeed, for those who have ears to hear, the whole movement is a perfect proof of the assertion that the classical concerto, with its recurrent buttressing tutti, solves the problems which faced Bach and Mozart alike, by adapting to the classical view certain eternal principles which in an earlier age had resulted in the aria form and the *ritornello* concerto-movement.

The first movements of the following concertos are among those which may profitably be studied on the lines indicated:

Mozart	Pianoforte concertos, K.413, 414, 415, *450*, 453, 459, 467, 482, *488*, *491*, *503*, 537, 595. Those in italics are specially recommended.
	Clarinet concerto, K.622
Beethoven	Pianoforte concertos nos. 4 and 5
	Violin concerto
	Triple concerto
Brahms	Pianoforte concertos nos. 1 and 2
	Violin concerto
	Double concerto

Of the middle and final movements of the classical concertos it is not necessary to say much. The slow movements provide ideal opportunities for exploiting the lyrical capacity of solo instruments with the orchestra playing a subordinate rôle: for decorative embroidery by the solo of matter whose basis is orchestral: and for the alternation of solo and tutti in an antiphonal way which is too sectional in feeling to be suitable for the high organisation of the first movement. The combination and alternation of these functions of the soloist have produced many exquisite slow movements written in forms suitable to lyric expression.

The finales are usually rondos of the more highly-organised 'open' type. Strange to say, those of Beethoven and Brahms, though more weighty, are at bottom less subtly organised than Mozart's concerto-rondos, which have a most disconcerting way of confounding the expectations of the unwary listener and of the pundit. These rondos are, of course, much less relentless than the first movements in their calls upon the listener's attention.

4. The post-classical concerto.

Leaving aside the type of concerto written by virtuosi for virtuosi (like those of Paganini, for example), which have little musical value and are designed exclusively to display technical skill, we see in the post-classical musical world compositions for solo with orchestra of various kinds, all of a less subtle quality than the classical type. The reasons which led Schumann and Mendelssohn, for example, to abandon the opening tutti as 'redundant', and to concentrate more upon content and less upon form, are perfectly valid ones viewed in the light of the whole romantic outlook on art and life; and it would be unfair and absurd to hold that these composers are to be blamed on this account. On the other hand, having conceded this, we must recognise that the romantic concerto-forms, whether (like Mendelssohn's), paying tribute to the anatomical facts of sonata-form, or (like Liszt's) abandoning them for large fantasia-like attempts to put three movements into one, must of necessity be sectional, less subtly-organised structures than the classical concertos, since they solve the problem of reconciling the individual and the mass by ignoring its existence; solo and tutti may alternate, may embroider and accompany one another, but they cannot fuse. Tovey puts the matter in a nutshell when he says,[45] 'In the classical concerto forms, the orchestra and solo are so organised that both are at their highest development. The conditions of such a problem do not admit of many obviously different solutions; and the concertos that abandon the classical form obtain their unlimited variety by being structures of a much looser and less ambitious order'. This description will cover most concertos written after Beethoven's time, with the exception of those of Brahms.

[45] *Essays in Musical Analysis,* vol. III, p. 27.

VIII

VARIATION

VARIATION, IN THE technical musical sense, is a process whereby a complete musical entity (phrase, sentence, paragraph) is subjected, upon repetition, to elaboration or alteration of detail, while its essentials are retained so as to make it possible to recognise a point-to-point correspondence between the original and the variant forms; the latter point constitutes an essential difference between 'variation' and 'development'.

Among the forms already discussed, examples abound of the recapitulation or repetition of themes in varied forms; mention has been made of C. P. E. Bach's passion for decoration of this kind. In lyrical forms, such varied returns of important themes can play a great part in maintaining and increasing the interest; in sonata form, on the other hand, where interest arises mainly from the emphasis upon dramatic incident, there is rarely leisure to concentrate upon such artistic luxuries, and varied returns are usually a waste of both composer's and listener's time.

The mere harmonisation of a theme originally given out in unison is an example of variation, as may be seen, for example, in the 'Agnus Dei' of Verdi's *Requiem,* or in the 1st movement of Bach's *Clavier concerto in D minor* which was analysed in the last chapter; compare the A minor statement of the ritornello theme at bars 56-62 with the opening statement, bars 1-7. Or the simplest kind of figuration of the original harmonies may be employed to add cumulative interest to returns of a rondo-theme, as in the slow movement of Beethoven's piano sonata, op. 13, in which compare bars 1-8 with bars 9-16, and these two forms of the same sentence with 51-58 and 59-66. A slightly more elaborate instance of the same thing may be seen in the finale of the piano sonata op. 79 at bars 1-16, 35-50, and 72-95; the last contains within itself two variant forms of the original, so that in the whole movement four different simple figurations of the same harmony are found accompanying the rondo-theme.

This purely decorative type of variation found great favour with the romantic composers, especially those with a genius for piano-writing, who found their favourite instrument, with its immense and easily-controlled possibilities, ideally adapted to the purpose. Chopin's music, in particular, is rich in decorative variant treatment of his returns; examples occur throughout his work, the following being a few noteworthy ones:

Nocturne in E flat (op. 9 no. 2), bars 1-4, 5-8, 13-16, 21-24 (progressively more elaborate melodic decoration).

Nocturne in C minor (op. 48 no. 1), bars 1-24 and 49-72. (Variation of the entire main section of an episodical form.)

Sonata in B minor, finale, bars 9-28, 100-119, 206-225; (varied returns of rondo theme with progressively elaborate figuration of the harmony).

Having described and illustrated the *principle* of musical variation, we have now to consider those musical forms which are entirely based upon that principle. The early history of music shows that so long as composers had words to set, they were not at a loss to achieve continuity in pieces of considerable duration; the text, being a unity in itself, providing a satisfactory basis for reasonably large-scale musical forms. But so soon as the attempt was made to develop purely instrumental music (and this applies all over the world, in primitive and sophisticated societies alike) the problem at once arose, what to do next? (See page 9.) The crude answer to this question is, 'Play it over again', and the monotony of the result no doubt led almost at once to the adoption of means of adding interest to these repetitions. Hence we find folk-forms like the *piobaireachd* of the Scottish Highlands sharing with all kinds of oriental musical forms the vital characteristic of extempore (and almost endless) melodic elaborations of a definite theme. The instrumental music of the composers of the sixteenth century shows that, in a far more self-conscious way, they naturally adopted the same means of making their music last more than a minute or two. Indeed, until subtler means of organisation had been achieved by the continuous development and experimentation of the seventeenth-century composers, the only alternatives to variation-writing were the stringing together of numbers of small pieces as in the suites and 'sonate', or the use of essentially vocal forms like the motet form for the purposes of instrumental music (as in the peculiarly English form, the *Fancy*).

Sixteenth-century instrumental composers developed two distinct variation-types; one in which a short theme (usually in the bass) was repeated continuously without break, while the harmony, melody and figuration were subjected to progressive variation; and the other in which a self-contained theme, with a well-defined full-close, was made the basis of a series of independent little pieces, each a variation of the original. The more skilful composers, such as William Byrd, brought to the latter method a heightened sense of form and continuity by arranging the variations in such a way as to lead through increasing stages of elaboration to definite climaxes in the form of particularly complex or weighty variations.

It will be convenient at this point to separate these two basic methods of applying the variation-principle, and to consider them individually.

1. The recurrent-bass principle. *(Ground bass, basso ostinato)*

We need not consider the earliest origins of this principle beyond noting the names of the now forgotten dances, the *passacaglia* and the *ciaconna* or *chaconne,* whose music was undoubtedly written on a recurrent or *ground* bass. We must remember these two names, because it has become customary to use them in a rather loose sense as implying simply any piece in ground-bass form. All attempts to define the difference between *passacaglia* and *chaconne* are fruitless in the face of the somewhat indiscriminate use of the terms by the composers themselves.

A small number of ground-basses will be found in the Elizabethan virginal books (one by Thomas Tomkins has 45 variations), and a very much larger number in the works of the Italian composers of the first part of the seventeenth century; the latter introduced the form into vocal as well as instrumental works. Our first examples, however, are from the more developed and mature Purcell, with whom the ground-bass form was a prime favourite.

Look first at the glorious and well-known 'Lament' from *Dido and Aeneas*. The theme:

Ex. 13

is one of many variants of the phrase embodying a dropping fourth which was a great favourite for compositions of the kind. Purcell's genius has drawn over his 5-bar chromatic theme a vocal line of the most exquisite subtlety, in which the phrases are by no means all five bars long, but are so adjusted with little instrumental 'breathing spaces' as to bring voice and orchestra together at all important cadences. (See, e.g., the 14th bar.) More wonderful than this, however, is the highly-charged emotional atmosphere produced by the composer's use of the chromatic steps of the theme as the foundation of harmonies whose pathos has scarcely been surpassed in the whole of musical history. The student, after examining Dido's Lament, should also give close attention to the chorus 'Crucifixus' from Bach's *Mass in B minor*. Bach's theme is very similar to Purcell's, and he achieves his almost unbearable pathos by exactly the same means, i.e., the skilful use of suspensions and appoggiaturas over a slow chromatic descent, to create emotional tension.

Next, examine another ground-bass from *Dido and Aeneas,* the aria 'Ah, Belinda! I am prest with torment'. This piece, in an entirely different way, is almost as great a triumph as the Lament, the utmost technical ingenuity being used for the highest musical ends. The theme is very straightforward, of four bars, with a full-close at its end; yet the phrasing of the vocal line is as varied and free as if it were not bound by any restrictions at all. At the very outset Purcell contrives, by starting his voice a bar later than his bass, to make two repetitions of the bass cover a *7-bar* vocal sentence; this sentence is not, as one might expect, built up of a 3-bar phrase followed by a 4-bar one, with cadences coinciding with those of the bass, but the exact opposite. In other words, the last bar of the first vocal phrase comes in contact with the *first* bar of the bass theme, while the second vocal phrase covers bars 2-4 of the bass, making bass and treble coincide again. (See. Ex. 14.)

Ex. 14

The next ten bars are even more astonishing. (Ex. 15.)

Ex. 15

Here we have first a 4-bar vocal phrase coinciding with the bass, followed by a *5-bar* vocal phrase which overlaps into the next repetition of the bass, to be followed at once by a return to the beginning, and repetition of as much of the aria as we have heard so far. Since the aria began (Ex. 14) with a 3-bar phrase, this once more brings bass and voice together.

Turn next to bar 36. Here, after the voice has been silent for two bars, it re-enters with the beginning of its phrase *on the last bar of the bass theme.* (That this is an anticipation of the bass-theme itself, giving the bass the effect of imitating the voice, is a purely incidental example of Purcell's superb sense of musical craftsmanship.)

We now have a 4-bar vocal phrase *which does not coincide with the* 4-bar bass-theme, in effect using the third bar of the latter to make a half-close. The voice being now, as it were, a bar ahead of the bass, it restores equilibrium with a glorious extension of the phrase just sung, into one of 5 bars. (Ex. 16.)

Ex. 16

The bass is thereafter given two repetitions in the dominant key, after which it returns to the tonic. The student must examine the rest of the piece for himself; it contains further rhythmic subtleties fully as striking as those illustrated.

We may next notice Bach's immense *Passacaglia* for organ, on an 8-bar theme with a half-close at the fourth bar and a full-close at the eighth. The work shows all Bach's contrapuntal skill and endless resource, though it is noticeably less enterprising than the Purcell works discussed above in the matter of rhythmic subtlety, sticking closely as it does to the 4-bar pattern indicated by the bass. Nevertheless it surely transcends all previous works in the form, in the variety of figuration adopted in its 20 variations, and above all in the consummate skill with which these variations are grouped together. Some are more highly-developed versions of their predecessors, so as to provide a larger architectural satisfaction in the placing of climaxes, in the variety of mood, and above all in the tremendous final work-up to a triumphant conclusion. All of this tends, as a matter of fact, to make an anti-climax of the fugue, founded on the bass-theme, which follows.

It will be noted that the bass is itself varied in a primitive way in variations 5, 9, 10 and 18, that it leaves the organ pedals and goes into the left-hand part at variations 14 and 15, and that variations 11-13 provide relief by taking the melody out of the ground into an upper or middle part of the counterpoint.

Bach's colossal *Chaconne* for unaccompanied violin, with its 64 variations upon a 4-bar theme, is another of the landmarks of the ground-bass form. Here, as in many chaconnes, the variations are as much upon the simple noble harmonies which accompany the bass at the outset as upon the bass itself.

The ground-bass found little favour with the true classical composers, who were perhaps too much preoccupied with the new problems and possibilities provided by the sonata form. A notable case of a set of variations which is in effect a chaconne, however, was provided by Beethoven in his *32 variations in C minor* for pianoforte, on a theme with a descending chromatic bass which, with its enormous harmonic possibilities, plays a much greater part in holding the piece together than does the actual tune. Let us study the outline of this well-known composition:

Theme:		An 8-bar sentence consisting of (a) a bass descending in 6 chromatic steps plus 2-bar cadence: (b) a set of harmonies: and (c) a melody travelling in general in contrary motion to the bass.
Vars.	1-3	A series of variations in which an arpeggio figure is worked first in the right hand, then in the left, and finally in both at once. The bass is as in the

theme, the harmonies remain substantially unaltered except for a very colourful substitution of a 'neapolitan' chord for a dominant at bar 3 of var. 3, and necessary subsequent modifications. Of the tune there is no sign.

The next three variations each work a separate figuration:

Var. 4 Bass and harmonies intact. No sign of the tune.

Var. 5 Purely harmonic connection with the theme, the chords being now in root position, and the bass as such absent. A remote connection with the main notes of the tune seems more a matter for the eye than for the ear.

Var. 6 Bass and harmonies intact. Melody absent.

Vars. 7-8 A pair, 8 being a development of 7 with identical left-hand part. The harmony provides the link with the theme, as in var. 5; the bass as such is missing, and there is no trace of the tune.

Var. 9 For the first time, the tune, in a highly expressive transformation, is clearly discernible. The bass is present for the first half, as are the original harmonies, after which both undergo considerable modification until the cadence. As if to counterbalance this, the melody is most clearly stated at this point.

Vars. 10-11 This pair works a strong rhythmic figure and a violent demisemiquaver one in a kind of free double counterpoint. In both, the harmonies provide the strongest link with the theme.

Vars. 12-14 Tonic major key, with the tune paramount, first in the treble, then in the bass in 2-part counterpoint, finally in the bass in thirds, with a running counterpoint in thirds also; 14 is a development of 13. Of the original bass there is no sign, while the harmonies, largely new and very rich in 12, are a secondary consideration in 13 and 14.

Vars. 15-16 A pair, 16 being only a slight rhythmic modification of 15. These two are really related to the theme at second-hand, being harmonically connected with the rich var. 12, and making little reference to the theme itself.

Var. 17 A marvellously expressive variation in which the right-hand treats the opening figure of the tune (now returned to the minor mode) in imitation, accompanied by a broken-chord formality which sustains the substance of the original harmony, though not of the bass. In the last two bars the hands exchange functions, to allow the imitations to descend right to the bottom of the keyboard.

Vars. 18-21 A series of highly dramatic variations with little melodic, but much rhythmic content; 20 and 21 being a pair of opposites like 10-11. In all four, the original harmony is substantially preserved, but there is little sign of the original bass until no. 20 when it appears as the treble part for the first half. In no. 18 the melody can be heard distinctly in the accented notes at the top of each scale.

Var. 22 A 2-part canon at the octave below, ingeniously contrived to preserve the harmonic basis of the theme.

Var. 23 The bass appears again intact, for the first time since var. 9. This variation depends entirely on the bass and the harmony (wonderfully coloured by an inverted dominant pedal for 6 bars) for its effect, as well as for its connection with the theme.

Vars. 24-25 Two individuals, each working a particular figure. The bass is largely absent in 24, but present in very strict form in 25. The harmonies, substantially intact in 24, are rigorously adhered to in 25 which, in fact, is one of the strictest of the set, though utterly different from the theme in character.

Vars. 26-27 A pair of highly rhythmic variations, in both of which the outline of the tune is discernible for the first time since 18. The bass is absent from both, but the harmonies remain, such modifications as there are (as at bars 4-5) being common to both.

Var. 28 A new cantabile melody spun over an 'Alberti bass' which covers the harmonies of the theme without reproducing its bass.

Var. 29 Harmonies and original bass reproduced in violent arpeggio-figuration.

Var. 30 Lull before the storm. The original bass supports harmonies which are a colourful extension of the original ones. The treble reminds one of the tune in its now quite methodical contrary motion, but it is doubtful whether the ear can appreciate its closeness to the original.

Vars. 31-32 A pair, the left-hand parts being identical. Starting *pp* over a tonic-pedal which lasts throughout both, the melody is given intact in no. 31, but gives way except in outline on the first of each bar in no. 32 to a rushing of scales which now increase from the *pp* to a furious *ff*, on which the coda starts. Both variations preserve the original harmonies, with but slight differences.

Coda Of considerable dimensions, containing after 11 bars of tremendous momentum, another almost complete variation (harmonies and bass close to the theme), whose 7th bar introduces the *melodic figure* of the 7th bar of the theme in contrary motion between treble and bass. This is developed for 8 bars, and leads to the final formalities lasting a further 18 bars, in which the initial figure of the tune plays a considerable part.

This superbly original composition serves well as a link between the ground-bass section of this chapter and the section which follows, illustrating as it does, many of the more straightforward ways of varying a self-contained theme. It remains only to say of the ground-bass that it has come into favour again in the twentieth century, having been largely ignored in the nineteenth except for certain superb specimens by Brahms and Rheinberger. As may be supposed, modern composers treat it with very considerable freedom, but the later examples in the following list of works (which is roughly chronological) will repay study, analysis and close attention quite as much as the earlier.

Purcell *King Arthur,* act IV. An enormous passacaglia which, with the exception of a short duet, covers the whole music of the act. It is in 59 variations, divided as follows:

1. Orchestral prelude, 14 variations on the bass, of which 9-10 are on a free inversion.
2. Soprano solo, 4 variations, the last overlapping
3. Chorus, 4 variations; an expansion of (2)
4. Orchestral interlude, 11 variations, some on the inverted bass.
5. Duet for soprano and bass, 10 variations of which the 6th has an extra bar which twists into the relative major and out again.

6. Chorus, 5 variations.
7. Trio, female voices. 2 variations on the inverted theme plus two 'free' variations modulating to the dominant.
8. Trio, male voices, 3 variations.
9. Trio, female voices, 2 variations.
10. Choral expansion of (9), 2 variations.

Handel	*Passacaglia in G minor—Lessons, (1st set, no. 7)*
	Chaconne in G—Lessons, (2nd set, no. 9)
Bach	*Clavier concerto in D minor,* 2nd movt., (in which each variation is in a different key, with 2- or 3-bar modulating links separating one from another)
	Church cantata no. 78, opening chorus. (A superb example, in which the Chaconne is combined with line-by-line treatment of the chorale tune.)
Rheinberger	*Passacaglia in E minor;* from *Organ Sonata no. 8.*
Brahms	Finale of the *Variations on a theme of Haydn.*
	Finale of *Symphony no. 4* (in which the theme is given out as the *treble* of a mass of harmony, and only after 3 variations descends to the bass. Here also a novel element is introduced by the recapitulation, from variation 24, of the earliest variations, giving the movement a sense of solidity befitting its position).
Max Reger	*Passacaglias in D minor* and *E minor* for organ.
Vaughan Williams	Finale of *Symphony no. 5.*
Bloch	Finale of *String quartet no. 2* (bars 79-225).
Britten	Finale of *String quartet no. 2.*

2. *Variations upon a self-contained theme*

The analysis, in the previous section, of Beethoven's *32 Variations in C minor* should have given the student a considerable idea of the resources upon which a skilful composer may call in writing variations; these resources are bounded only by the composer's powers of technique and imagination, and we shall see that variation writing has called forth several of the greatest masterpieces in the whole of music.

It has been mentioned that the sixteenth-century virginal composers were fond of the form, and a glance through some of their works will amply demonstrate the fact. Byrd's famous *Carman's Whistle* and also other pieces of his such as *O Mistress Mine, The Woods so Wild* and *John come kiss me now* are good examples of the method of increasingly elaborate accompaniments to a tune which is always well to the fore; a method which Farnbay, Bull, Morley and others followed also.

In the instrumental music of the century which followed, the focus is rather upon the slow development of more continuous forms; the main interest of variation-writing lies in ground-basses, and sets of formal self-contained variations are few except for the type known as 'doubles', which are variants of dance-tunes in the instrumental suites, in which as a rule the time-unit of the original is subdivided into successively smaller particles. Handel's keyboard lessons contain several such sets of 'doubles', a notable and famous instance being the air known as *The Harmonious Blacksmith.* Examples also occur in Bach's suites, such as the 2nd courante in the *English Suite no. 1.* 'Doubles' usually retain the original melodic outline rather carefully, and are thus, like the virginals sets, variations of a relatively lowly kind; the interest lying chiefly in the varied figuration of the accompaniment.[46]

Of a higher order altogether is that type of variation in which the basic *harmony* of the theme is the element common to each variation. Such sets are, of course, closely allied to the ground-bass forms; and it is sometimes a moot point (as in the case of the Beethoven set in C minor) whether they should be classified as ground-basses or as sets of variations.

The first truly monumental work in variation-form is of this kind—Bach's set of 30 for double-manual harpsichord known as the *'Goldberg' variations.* An exhaustive examination of this work is impossible here, and the student is referred to Tovey's masterly essay.[47] The essential point is

[46] 'Doubles' (though not so-styled) are found so late as Beethoven, as for instance in the middle movements of his *pianoforte sonatas op. 14 no. 2* and *op. 57.*

[47] *Essays in Musical Analysis—Chamber Music,* p. 28.

that we should understand how Bach's extremely regularly-constructed sarabande provides the foundation for the extraordinarily varied collection of self-contained pieces which follows. The melody of the theme plays no part in the variations. Nor with any regularity does the bass *as such,* though parts of it are to be found in innumerable places. Rather we have to regard the bass of the theme as being the foundation of harmonies, not in themselves immutable, and these harmonies as the factor common to the theme and to all the variations. Once this is clear, there can be no difficulty in following the connection between theme and variations throughout. What is staggering about this composition is its variety of mood, the immensity of its emotional range, and of course, the technical means by which these are secured. It is not sufficient to remark with wonder upon the fact that every third variation is a canon, the intervals of the canons increasing each time from the unison to the ninth. After all, it is not so very difficult to write a canon; but each of these canons is in itself a perfectly wrought piece of music, each an individual different from any of the others, and yet each bound to the theme. Then, many of the variations are in the form of virtuoso-pieces exploiting particular aspects of keyboard-technique with an artistry and musical integrity of the kind found in Chopin's *Etudes.* Such are nos. 5, 8, 11, 14, 17, 20, 23, 26, 28 and 29 (almost, again, every third one). Most of the remaining variations are in some specific form or dance-rhythm: thus nos. 13 and 25 are exquisite examples of Bach's *cantilene* style: no. 10 is a fughetta, no. 16 a French Overture with *grave* and fugal allegro, while others are in the form of minuet, courante and gigue. The last of all is a 'quodlibet' or pot-pourri of popular tunes of Bach's day.

In his *Chorale-partitas* and *Variations in the Italian manner* Bach left other sets of variations, but on the whole they lack abiding interest. An exception may perhaps be made in the case of the variations on the Chorale 'Vom Himmel hoch'; yet there will be few to deny that these are notable rather as a *tour de force* of contrapuntal ingenuity than as music.

During the classical period of Haydn and Mozart, variation writing was one of the favourite methods of composition, and both masters produced many sets, either as works complete in themselves, or as movements in string quartets, sonatas, and so on. While it would be true to say that no set of variations comparable in scope to Bach's 'Goldberg' set was written before Beethoven's late period, most of Haydn's sets and some of Mozart's are fine pieces of music, while something is to be learned even from the rather facile type of variation which Mozart sometimes produced. Such a set is that upon the nursery-tune, 'Ah! vous dirai-je, Maman' (known to us as 'Twinkle, twinkle, little star'). Pleasant, never straying far from the melodic outline of the tune or from the original harmonies; occasionally moving into the minor for a variation or two, now using some simple imitative counterpoint of the kind which Mozart could invariably make effective in an effortless way.

The set which opens Mozart's extremely well-known *Pianoforte sonata in A major (K.331),* while displaying the same attitude to the form (i.e., it is an elegant series of decorations of the original without much attempt at musical coherence of a larger kind) is on a higher plane of artistry, inasfar as the decoration is of a less perfunctory nature. Without much difficulty we can imagine the sort of variations that some musical hack might have written upon this theme, had he had no higher object in view than Mozart's—the amusing of a few ladies in a Paris salon; and by that imaginary yardstick we can measure the value of those which Mozart actually did write.[48] Examining the movement, we find that every one of the six variations sticks closely to the outline of the actual melody of the theme, including that in the minor key (no. 3) and that in which the time is altered from

[48] I am unable to understand the present fashion of decrying this movement. It seems to me to fulfil its unpretentious conditions to perfection.

compound to simple (no. 6). With the possible exception of the last, however, the decoration is in each case full of character and individuality, variation 5 being a notably beautiful example of simple cantabile tracery. Throughout the set, the harmony of the original remains virtually unchanged, such minor modifications as exist being entirely in the nature of changes of inversion, and usually simplifications of the original at that.

Mozart probably brought the simple decorative type of variation to its highest pitch in the last movement of his *Pianoforte concerto in C minor (K.491).* It is a movement fully able to hold its place in that superb work, although in matters of technical method it is not greatly in advance of the A major set just discussed. Mozart has here, of course, the stimulus of the great variety of orchestral colour at his disposal, which of itself is an important factor in variation-writing, and which can give rise to effects of antiphony and contrast which are impossible upon a single instrument.

Haydn, besides writing sets of variations on the decorative principle, just as naïve as anything from Mozart's pen (for example the well-known 'Emperor' variations in his string quartet op. 76 no. 3), developed a special variation-form which (apart from one or two not dissimilar movements in Beethoven) has remained uniquely his own. This form appears in many movements of his larger works, but is nowhere better displayed than in the famous *Variations in F minor* for pianoforte. The principle is that of having *two* alternating themes, a minor and a major, which are both given out before either is varied. There follow alternate variations upon each theme, the process seldom going beyond the second variation upon the first theme. The work is then rounded off with a coda on the grand scale, developed from the material of the first theme. This coda gives Haydn's variation-form a strength and unity which are absent from Mozart's variations, but which is found again in Beethoven and Brahms. Let us examine the Haydn *Variations in F minor* more closely:

1. A 29-bar theme in simple open 2-part form, key F minor.
2. A 20-bar theme similarly constructed, key F major.
3. A variation of (1), subtly and skilfully contrived on the decorative principle.
4. A variation of (2), much closer to the original; indeed, really only an ornamented version of its original.
5. A more elaborate variation of (1).
6. A more elaborate variation of (2), the first part shortened by 2 bars.
7. Restatement of (1), breaking off at the 22nd bar into:
8. Coda, 61 bars in length, of great power and originality. It develops the characteristic figure of the first theme, and even, as was Beethoven's practice, includes an additional variation of part of the second half of theme (1).

Further examples of Haydn's alternating-variation form:

Pianoforte sonata in C sharp minor,[49] second movement (a simple example.)
Pianoforte sonata in E,[50] last movement (in which the first theme returns each time in its original form, but is varied at the repetitions.)
Pianoforte sonata in D,[51] last movement.
Pianoforte sonata in G,[52] 1st movement.
String quartet op. 55 no. 2, 1st movement.
String quartet in E flat, op. 71 no. 3, 2nd movement.
Symphony no. 103 ('Drumroll'), 2nd movement.

Beethoven raised the art of variation writing to an artistic level which has never been surpassed, and he made it the vehicle for some of the most beautiful and profound things that have ever been said in music. Such, for example, are the slow movements of the 9th symphony and of the last piano sonata, op. 111. He wrote innumerable sets, both independent and as movements in sonatas, chamber works and symphonies. They range from easy pot-boilers (like the set on 'Rule, Britannia') to the glories of the choral variations in the finale of the 9th symphony; and from the quiet simplicity

[49] Augener no. 6; new Peters (ed. Martienssen) no. 6; old Peters (ed. Ruthardt) no. 6.
[50] Augener no. 10; Martienssen no. 40; Ruthardt no. 34.
[51] Augener no. 14; Martienssen no. 20; Ruthardt no. 19.
[52] Augener no. 16; Martienssen and Ruthardt no. 10.

of the slow movement of the 'Appassionata' sonata to the subtleties and complexities of the *'Diabelli' variations* for pianoforte, which is one of Beethoven's greatest works, and the most important set of variations ever written.

In discussing Beethoven's variations, we need not consider the vapid salon-pieces which, following the execrable fashion of the early nineteenth century, no doubt served to bring him needed ducats. The more seriously-conceived sets show an attitude to the form which, though suggested in Haydn's more important variations, is to all intents and purposes new—that of treating the theme not as a foundation to be subjected to different forms and degrees of elaboration, but as a simple framework upon which a series of developed musical entities shall be built; the series so arranged as to provide climaxes and recessions of feeling, whereby a larger unity is achieved. Thus Beethoven's finer sets are creations of a far higher order of artistic achievement than could ever be attained by the mere haphazard stringing together of decorated versions of the theme.

Beethoven regards his theme from three standpoints: that of the tune or melody, that of the harmony, and that of the rhythm (i.e., of the detailed phrase-structure). His variations may concentrate upon any one or any two, or on all three of these aspects with the result that he has at command a far more flexible apparatus than had Bach, who was tied to the harmony, or Mozart, who was tied to the melody. Furthermore, this conception of the theme allows of variation in ways which may seem superficially to wander far from the original—a point seized upon by Beethoven on the wider structural ground that by careful arrangement of easily-recognisable variations and more obscure ones, he could bring greater variety and contrast into his work.

The set which opens the well-known *Pianoforte sonata in A flat (op. 26)* may be taken first as exemplifying Beethoven's variation-writing in an early but perfectly mature state:

Theme: A simple 'closed' 3-part form. The first part is a sentence of two 4-bar phrases ending in a half-close, and repeated to end in a full-close. The second part begins with a 2-bar unit repeated in sequence a tone lower. Then a 4-bar phrase, seeming about to come to a full-close in the dominant, has instead an interrupted cadence, and is then extended by two further bars of cadential repetition, full-close in the dominant, and lead into the third part, which is virtually identical with the repeated form of the first.

The exact detail of this structure is followed throughout the five variations, with the exception that in no. 3 the first sentence is not easily broken into two phrases, and the downward sequence which opens the second part is greater than one step. This very fact is, of course, itself evidence of structural variation.

Var. 1 While the harmony is a replica of the original, the melodic outline is concealed in the characteristic figure of the variation in a remarkably subtle way, seeming continually to remind one of the melody of the theme without doing more than to suggest it. The second part is frankly decorative, the melody being present.

Var. 2 Among characteristic figuration which is used consistently throughout, the melody is to be heard in a middle part. The harmony undergoes no substantial change, though many chords are in new inversions.

Var. 3 In the tonic minor key. The melody is recognisable only occasionally as at bars 1-2, 23-26. The harmony, while preserving the main features of the original, introduces some quite new chords as at the 4th, 7th, 21st and 22nd bars. This variation is a remarkable illustration of the gulf which lies between Mozart's and Beethoven's conception of the scope of the subject.

Var. 4 In the first part, the melodic outline of the original is transformed into something so different that it is hard to see it at first, though the ear traces the connection without difficulty. Melodic connection virtually disappears in the second part. The harmony undergoes much change of position, some radical alteration, and a curious anticipatory treatment at bars 5-8.

Var. 5 A very straightforward decorative variation, in which the repeats and returns are themselves further decorated. The harmony is as in the theme, and the melody is clearly audible.

Coda 15 bars unconnected with the theme, except inasfar as the bass may be held to be derived from its first bar.

Before proceeding further, the student will be well advised to analyse carefully some of the following sets of Beethoven's variations, in which the technique employed is of the same order as in the work just described:

Variations in F, op. 34. Nominally 6 variations, but actually 7, as the coda contains a complete variation. The time of each variation is different, and (quite exceptionally) the key of each is a third lower than that of its predecessor.

15 variations, op. 35. Known as the 'Prometheus' variations. A remarkable set, in which the *bass* of the theme is first given; only after three variations upon the bass, with increasingly elaborate counterpoint, have been heard, is the theme itself played. Well worth very close study indeed.

String quartet in A, op. 18 no. 5 (3rd movement.)

Sonata in A, op. 47, for violin and piano ('Kreutzer'), 2nd movement.

Clarinet trio, op. 11 (finale)

Septet, op. 20 (4th movement.)

In his third period, Beethoven may be said to have developed the same technique to its limit as a means of the highest possible musical expression. The *33 Variations on a theme of Diabelli (op. 120),* show the composer at his greatest.[53] Our purpose will be served by examining the set which forms the last movement of the *Pianoforte sonata in E (op. 109).* Thereafter, the student may seek for himself among the inexhaustible joys of the other sets of variations from Beethoven's late period, some of which are listed below.

Theme A simple open 2-part form in two sentences of eight bars, each repeated. The first part closes at bar 4 into the dominant, and again more firmly at bar 8. The second part, leaning strongly at bar 12 into G sharp minor (the mediant), returns at once to give the last 4 bars in the tonic. Threefold downward sequential movement at 9-12.

[53] The student is strongly advised to study these variations in conjunction with Tovey's analysis in his *Essays in Musical Analysis —Chamber Music* p. 124.

Var. 1 The melody of the theme entirely absent in the first part, recognisable in the 2nd. The harmony is simplified as compared with the original, the real bass moving much more slowly. The structure is maintained intact.

Var. 2 A 'double' variation; that is, the repeats are themselves new variations. Thus bars 33-40 and 49-56 form, as it were, one variation in which the characteristic figuration allows the melody of the theme to be easily recognised; bars 41-48 and 57-64 form another quite different variation in which the theme is present only as the initial idea of the figure which is worked imitatively, and again during the last 4 bars. In the first of these variants, bass and harmony are strictly faithful to the original. In the second, there is considerable modification and simplification of the harmonic basis, 41-47 being on a dominant pedal.

Var. 3 Change to duple time. Another double variation, but here the repeats are not completely distinct variations, being rather developments of one another. For 4 bars the original melody and bass are traceable in each other's places. The next four invert this counterpoint, restoring bass and treble as such. The following 8 bars are a varied form of this piece of double counterpoint. The second part is on similar lines, but in reverse order, the treble starting off with the original melodic outline, to be followed after 4 bars by the bass. The repeat then reverses this *in toto*.

Var. 4 Change to compound triple time and very slow tempo. The first part is contrapuntal in texture, the second part less so. There is no sign of the original melody except for a trace in the last few bars. The harmony is a reduction of the original to its lowest terms, the interest lying in the polyphony.

Var. 5 In quick duple time. A double variation of the same kind as var. 3, the repeats being developments of the first statements. The texture is severely contrapuntal, on a figure derived from the first two bars of the theme, in close imitation. The counterpoint becomes more elaborate as the variation proceeds. Both bass and harmony of the original are adhered to fairly consistently; the melody of the last 4 bars is recognisably that of the theme. The second part is here repeated *twice* with a difference only of dynamics.

Var. 6 A special type of continuously developing variation. Each 4 bars, the basic idea of the variation is speeded up and developed, there being thus (it being a double variation inasfar as there are no formal repeats) eight stages of development. Beginning quietly, bass and melody are distinctly as in the theme. At the repetition these are given in a decorated version, but are no less clear. An inverted dominant pedal which accompanies the first 6 bars, changing at the 7th bar to tonic, speeds up with each change of texture, becoming ultimately quite frankly a trill. For the second part, the dominant pedal goes into the bass, the right hand in demisemiquaver movement giving a version of the harmony of the theme in which the melodic outline is scarcely traceable. On repetition the roles are reversed, the right hand taking the trilled dominant pedal in the inner part, and giving at the top the outline of the theme in addition. The left hand supplies the harmony.

Coda The cadence of var. 6 is extended downwards for three bars of dominant harmony over a tonic pedal, through a continuous diminuendo and into a quiet, exact recapitulation of the theme, without repeats.

While such a bald description of the technical facts can given no idea of the supreme quality of the music of these variations, it should be useful as a proof that Beethoven achieves his greatest feats within the strict formal limits imposed upon him by his whole attitude to variation-writing. It may be observed as a point of great æsthetic importance that Beethoven never allows the melody of his theme to be completely obscured for very long, alternating those variations which pay no heed to it with others in which it is clearly audible. The effect of this upon the listener's powers of attention to the more 'difficult' variations is of great importance.

Other late Beethoven variations:

Pianoforte sonata in C minor (op. 111), (2nd movement).
String quartet in E flat (op. 127), (2nd movement.) A hard nut to crack.
String quartet in C sharp minor (op. 131), (4th movement).
String quartet in F (op. 135), (3rd movement).
Pianoforte trio in B flat (op. 97), (3rd movement).

Before leaving the subject of Beethoven's variations, it is

necessary to draw attention to the movements, so thoroughly characteristic of him, which are not sets of variations in the orthodox sense of the word. First there is the finale of the 3rd Symphony, a movement quite unique in its blend of variations (upon the same theme as op. 35 for pianoforte), fugal writing and episodical matter. Then there are the choral variations which form the finale of the 9th Symphony, some of which are strict, while in others the theme is the foundation of self-contained movements not complying with the details of the theme's structure. Finally, there are several sets in which something akin to Haydn's alternating-theme principle can be seen; probably none of them can be said to correspond to Haydn's form exactly, though the slow movement of the piano trio in E flat, op. 70 no. 2, comes very near to it. On similar lines, but each unique in itself and well worth studying for its own sake, are the following:

Symphony no. 5, 2nd movement.
Symphony no. 7, 2nd movement.
Symphony no. 9, 3rd movement.
String quartet in A minor (op. 132), 3rd movement.

Of the later masters, the only one whose variation-writing is in any way comparable to Beethoven's is Brahms. He cannot be said to have added anything fundamental to the resources of classical variation-writing, for Beethoven had thoroughly explored its possibilities; but with a complete understanding of Beethoven's mature method, Brahms brought to it the qualities of emotional warmth and advanced instrumental technique which were his own, as well as the increased harmonic resources which the romantic composers had developed. The student who has carefully studied some of the Beethoven variation-movements listed above will require no further guidance; his earlier trouble will be rewarded by his delight at each new discovery of the beauties and ingenuities of Brahms's work.

A particularly dramatic view of the progress of variation-writing over a century-and-a-half may be obtained by making a comparison between Handel's little set of variations in the first of his second set of Harpsichord lessons with the enormous work by Brahms on the same theme (op. 24), a work worthy to rank with the Goldberg and Diabelli sets.

Some important variation-movements by Brahms:

On a theme of Schumann, for pianofore duet (op. 23).
On a theme of Haydn, for orchestra or two pianos (op. 56).
On an original theme (op. 21 no. 1).
On a Hungarian theme (op. 21 no. 2).
On a theme of Handel (op. 24).
On a theme of Paganini (op. 35). (Two complete sets, in the form of studies which exploit the furthest resources of the piano.)
String quartet in B flat (op. 67), last movement.
Clarinet quintet (op. 115), last movement.
String sextet in B flat (op. 18), 2nd movement.
String sextet in G (op. 36), 3rd movement.

Of the other nineteenth-century composers, only Schubert needs to be considered seriously as a writer of variations in the classical sense. His best sets, such as those in the *String quartet in D minor,* in the *'Wanderer' fantasia* for piano, and the B flat *Impromptu,* show the Mozartian attitude coloured by Schubert's own advanced harmonic daring, and by a strong sense of dramatic effect. Mendelssohn's few sets of variations are superficially decorative without showing Mozart's ability to stick to his text. Chopin's are elegant salon-pieces which only the composer's innate artistry raises above the level of the hordes of examples of decorative inanity which were fashionable in his day. Schumann's tend to be free self-contained pieces connected with the theme only by melodic reference to its main features, and in no sense adhering to its structure.

3. The so-called 'free' variation forms.

Mention of Schumann's variations brings us to the last section of this chapter, which is included only for the sake of completeness, since it has no real relevance to a discussion of variation writing in the classical sense. The tendency since Brahms's day (and in certain instances earlier, as with

Schumann) has been to regard the theme not as containing melodic, harmonic and structural elements to be varied without being destroyed, but as a kind of quarry from which may be dug material to serve as the basis of a series of pieces structurally quite independent of the theme, varied in length, shape and emotional scope. It is merely a matter of convenience that such series of pieces are called 'variations' at all. Works produced according to such a scheme can be very beautiful (like Elgar's *'Enigma' variations*) but they must of necessity be looser, and therefore lighter, structures (inasfar as they are structures in the wider sense at all) than the great classical sets, whose themes remain perpetually in the background as a unifying element. The 'free' variation series offers unlimited scope for ingenuity and artistry, but always on the restricted scale laid down by the individual formal requirements of each separate 'variation'. Among such sets, of varying quality, the following will be found worth study:

Elgar	*'Enigma' variations.*
Tchaikovsky	*Variations from orchestral suite no. 3 in G.*
Dvořák	*Symphonic Variations.*
Reger	*Variations on a theme of Mozart,* for orchestra.
Dohnányi	*Variations on a nursery theme* for piano and orchestra.
Britten	*Variations on a theme of Purcell* or *The Young Person's Guide to the Orchestra.*

IX

CONTRAPUNTAL FORMS

OF THE MANY definitions of 'counterpoint', Tovey's seems to be the most complete—'the conveying of a mass of harmony by means of a combination of melodies'.[54] By 'contrapuntal forms' we mean those musical forms which owe their existence to the application of counterpoint in special ways. Of such forms there are several classes, two of which must claim our attention in the present volume.

1. Fugue.

Such a mass of literature on the subject of fugue exists, from the minute detail of Prout's monumental volumes[55] to the succinct and admirable chapter in Morris's *The Structure of Music* that it is difficult to see the need for more than a description of some of the infinity of ways in which composers have applied the principles of fugue to their music. At the same time it is necessary to issue a warning against the kind of textbook (of which Cherubini's *Course of Counterpoint and Fugue* is the most notorious) which purports to lay down regulations as to the requirements of a properly-written fugue, and which is contradicted at every turn by the real music of the fugues of masters like Bach and Handel.

If we accept the implications of Tovey's definition of counterpoint, we can say that counterpoint is the *texture* of the musical fabric. *Fugue* is a particular form of that texture, in that the strands are woven according to a certain method; and *a fugue* is a piece of structurally self-sufficient music in which the fugal *method* is applied consistently throughout.[56]

[54] *Musical Articles from the* Encyclopædia Britannica, p. 30.

[55] *Fugue* and *Fugal Analysis*

[56] Bukofzer defines fugue in the modern sense as 'a contrapuntal form of the highest concentration in which a single characteristic subject in continuous expansion pervades a thoroughly unified whole'. (*Music in the Baroque Era,* p. 287).

Within this broad definition, the scope for variety is almost infinite; the only real way in which the student can come to realise just how immense it is, is for him to make a careful study of many examples of good fugues. If he were to undertake the labour of making a complete analysis of every fugue in Bach's '48', he would only be one of many who have derived incalculable benefit from that not-so-very-Herculean task.

Fugue originated in the early days of pure choral church music, with the very natural instinct of composers to bring in their voices in imitation of one another. The different *tessitura* of tenor and bass, treble and alto, naturally led to these imitations taking place at pitches separated by a fourth, a fifth or an octave. The demands of this early 'fuguing' were satisfied so soon as all voices employed in the composition had made their entry. The natural impulse to 'fugue' each clause of the words which were being set to music led ultimately to the perfection of the 'motet-form' of the sixteenth century, in which each clause is 'fugued' to a thematic scrap of its own, the new clause beginning, as a rule, by overlapping the cadence of the previous one. The composer thereby achieved continuity of expression, and was able by contrast to mark the end of important sections of his text by bringing all the voices to a close together and making a fresh start.

A well-known and easily-accessible example of this method is Orlando Gibbons's *Almighty and Everlasting God.*[57]

Bar 1 The bass opens the piece, to be followed at intervals of 4 beats by the alto at the octave above, the tenor at the fourth above, and finally the treble at the octave above the tenor.

Bar 6 As tenor and treble finish this clause, the alto enters with a new musical phrase to 'mercifully look upon our infirmities', to be followed this time in very close overlapped succession by bass, treble and tenor. This second clause is rather more highly developed than the

[57] The barring is that used in the *Tudor Church Music* octavo series (O.U.P.), reprinted in *The Church Anthem Book.*

first, in that a second series of entries in the reverse order of voices takes place, starting at bar 8, and in fact this is extended so that each voice sings the characteristic phrase twice, before the whole comes to a strong close at bar 11.

Bar 11 Rising out of this close again, begins a new figure in imitation to 'and in all our dangers and necessities'.

The process is repeated as follows:

Bar 15 'Stretch forth Thy right hand'

Bar 21 'to help and defend us' (as an independent clause)

Bar 25 'through Christ our Lord'.

The whole piece is rounded off with an elaborate 'Amen'.

Though this piece, technically speaking, is no doubt an 'anthem', being in the English language, it perfectly illustrates the earliest fully-developed ancestor of the modern 'fugue', and its principles apply to thousands of motets by Palestrina, Lasso, Victoria, Byrd, and other composers of the 'Golden Age'. Likewise, this method was applied to sections of setting of the Mass, and (with secular words) to many madrigals, both English and Italian. It also became the basis of the typical English instrumental form, the 'fantasy' or 'fancy'. Throughout the following century in England, while the Italians and Flemings were developing instrumental forms, the motet-form kept its grip, and so late as Purcell we find it extensively used. Purcell's *String Fantasias* of 1680, as well as much of his church music (e.g. the great *Jubilate* in *D major*) are among the last examples of the motet-form.

On the continent of Europe, during the first part of the seventeenth century, composers such as Sweelinck and Frescobaldi were feeling their way forward in their efforts to achieve extended instrumental forms. The *Ricercare,* the *Canzona* and the *Toccata* are transitional forms which bridge the gap between the motet and the mature fugue. All these tended to be sectional in construction, though often the sections were linked by being based upon rhythmic transformations of the same theme. In these forms were developed the countersubject in double counterpoint, the stretto, and most of the devices which lie to the hand of the composer who can make them subservient to his musical plan, and of the musical mathematician who regards them as an end instead of a means.

This process of development led to the supreme achievements of Bach and Handel. Without going into the matter of the background to their respective fugal styles too deeply, we may say that Handel represents the highest point of the Italian or Southern tradition; Bach that of the Northern, or Germanic; though of course, both traditions had common origins, and were continuously influencing one another. It is customary and convenient to study fugal structure by reference to Bach's works, and this practice we shall follow, noting in their place the main respects in which Handel tends to differ from Bach.

It should be observed first of all that a good fugue is *a good piece of music,* and that no amount of ingenious manipulation of contrapuntal devices will of itself make a basically bad design into a good one. One of the troubles about fugue has always been its appeal to those theorists and composers whose preoccupation with trees has prevented them from ever becoming aware of the existence of woods. The very nature of devices such as inversion, diminution, augmentation, stretto, double counterpoint and the rest is such that in the eyes and hands of these people they tend to become masters rather than servants; as a result, the very name 'fugue' has become associated in the minds of many listeners with pedantry and midnight oil.

Let us look into the question first in a general way, using examples from Bach's '48'.[58] II 12, if listened to purely as music without regard to technicalities, is a delightful piece in which a lively tune given out at the beginning is played twice more, each time at a lower pitch and in slightly more complex surroundings. Thereafter it makes its appearance periodically at the top, middle or foot of the counterpoint,

[58] For convenience we follow the reference-method used by Morris, I and II referring to the 1st and 2nd books of the '48', followed by the number of the fugue.

sometimes in a major key, sometimes in a minor; these appearances of the tune being divided from one another by pleasantly-wrought, euphonious 'free' sections in which occasionally a trace of the characteristic repeated first notes of the tune are to be heard. The attentive listener is aware that after an opening in which the sense of key is solidly grounded, the music enters a phase of greater variety of tonality, which is succeeded at the end by a short section where again the sense of fixed key is strong. No amount of scrutiny and analysis of the score of this fugue will reveal that it is essentially more complex than the above description implies.

Listen now to II 9. It is, in comparison with the previous example, a dignified and noble piece; but its slightly forbidding appearance in print will not blind the listener to the fact that its dignity and nobility are far from ponderousness or pedantry. Comparing his impression with that made by no. 12, he will be conscious of a greater degree of fulness of tone here, and will very probably realise that this is in part due to there being a great deal of 4-voice harmony as compared with the latter's maximum of three parts. He will notice in this case the different 'entries' of the opening tune coming at successively higher pitches, whereas in the other they appeared highest first, lowest last; and so soon as all are entered, he will probably be conscious of a 'closing-up' process, in which entries of the tune come hard on each other's heels; and the pleasure which he took in the alternation of 'free' passages with the entries of the tune as the piece progresses, will be replaced by interest in the varieties of effect which the composer obtains from such 'overlapped' entries in all manner of different positions and keys, scarcely leaving space for breath between; he will be conscious of a gradual increase of excitement, and if at his first hearing he notices that the composer has achieved this by doubling the speed of some of the overlapped entries, and even by turning some of these short quick entries upside-down, he may congratulate himself on his attentiveness to detail. Finally, he will be aware, as he was in no. 12, of a settling down of the harmony and an apparent drawing to a close.

We shall later analyse these two fugues in detail; but it should be clear by now that the *musical* essentials of fugue lie not in its technical detail, but in its adherence to the good psychological principles of firm statement, digression and re-establishment of solid ground which underlie all musical structures, both of the 'open' and the 'closed' types. Within this generalisation there is unlimited scope for variety, and once the student has firmly grasped the fact that the multifarious 'devices' of fugal writing are no more than the means by which this variety is attained, he may safely concentrate upon the study of technicalities.

The fugue, like the ritornello-form, was one of the main media of Bach's expression. Besides the '48', he wrote many glorious fugues for organ, innumerable vocal fugues of all kinds in his cantatas and other choral works, and countless other fugues scattered about his colossal output, whether as movements of suites or concertos, or as independent works, and whether actually styled fugues or not. His last work, *The Art of Fugue,* is a series of instrumental fugues on one theme, designed deliberately as a systematic exhibition of the scope of the fugue as an art-form. Its didactic purpose should not blind one to the magnificence of its music, and a careful study of it, along with Tovey's 'Companion to "The Art of Fugue"' (O.U.P.) is indispensible to a proper musical education.

Handel too, particularly in his great sacred works (though also elsewhere, both as to choral and as to instrumental fugues) found in fugue a natural mode of musical speech. Works like *Messiah* contain highly-developed fugues ('He trusted in God', 'Amen', 'His yoke is easy', 'And with his stripes we are healed'), as well as choruses containing substantial fugal sections. ('Hallelujah!', 'Glory to God'.)

Taking advantage of prior knowledge to save time, we shall now make certain statements about fugal construction, illustrate them, and leave the enquiring or sceptical student to verify them from the works of the great masters.

(a) *The exposition.*

'Exposition' is the term given to the opening section, in which all the voices sing the tune which is first of all given out by one of them. There is no rule as to the order in which they may enter, nor as to how many there shall be. Bach's tendency is to arrange the order so that each voice as it enters is either the highest or lowest for the time being; thus, by avoiding middle-voice entries to start with, he makes the listener's task easier. However, this is not a universal rule, as is shown by I 16, I 17, I 20, II 4 and II 22.

This opening tune, which normally contains melodic and/or rhythmic features of a kind which give it a strong character of its own, is called the *subject* of the fugue; when given by the next voice it is said to be *answered;* and ordinarily, the successive entries of the voices alternate between subject in the tonic key and answer in (or sometimes no more than *on;* see I 17) the dominant.

In about half the cases one meets, the answer is an exact transposition of the subject, and is known as a *real* answer; in all other cases there is some slight modification, and the answer is then a *tonal* one. Tonal answers are the result of a strong tendency to regard the scale as being divided into two complementary but unequal parts—tonic to dominant and dominant to tonic, and to answer prominent dominants in the subject by corresponding tonics, rather than supertonics, when the transposition of the subject to the dominant key takes place. The majority of tonal answers come into one of three categories:

(1) The subject begins on the dominant note, and the answer begins on the tonic, being thereafter adjusted to an exact transposition (ex. 17).

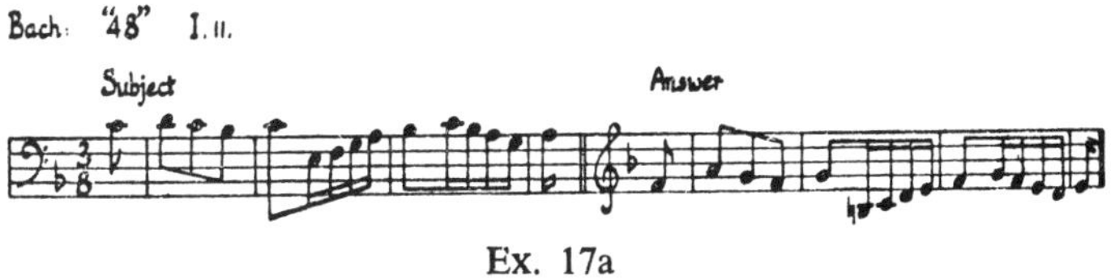

Ex. 17a

Ex. 17b

See also I 3, 12, 13 and 21; II 1, 2, 12, 14-17.

(2) The subject begins by moving from tonic to dominant, and is answered by a corresponding move from dominant to tonic; the remainder of the answer, as in (1), being an exact transposition to the dominant key (ex. 18).

Ex. 18 See also I 8, and 17; II 7.

It should be noted that this can apply even when the initial move from tonic to dominant is not a direct leap of the first two notes (ex. 19).

Ex. 19 See also I 2 and II 11.

(3) The third case is rarer, and is that of a subject which itself modulates from tonic to dominant, when the answer is so adjusted as to modulate from dominant to tonic (not to supertonic, as would be the case in an exact transposition.) No fugue in the '48' provides a simple illustration of this category, which is shown in the following from an organ fugue in C major (ex. 20).

Ex. 20

In I 7, however, we find an answer which is tonal both because it modulates *and* because it begins upon the dominant (ex. 21).

Ex. 21

I 18 and I 24 are other cases of the kind, with the additional point of interest that they illustrate the tendency to regard the new key as beginning so very early as almost to be answers at the *subdominant.*

The above rules cover the vast majority of cases in Bach's works, and to a lesser extent of Handel's also; the student who wishes to develop his technique and understanding of counterpoint by writing fugue in the Bach manner will be well advised to adhere to them. He must not, however, be surprised to find, in the works of these or of other masters, cases where they do not apply. Real answers are sometimes found where tonal ones might be expected, and answers are sometimes at the subdominant instead of the more usual dominant. The fugue from Bach's famous *Toccata in D minor* for organ, and the opening of Beethoven's *String quartet op. 131* are excellent illustrations of the latter point.

This short discussion of subject and answer would be incomplete without reference to certain procedures which lie outside the question of whether the answer is to be real or tonal, but whose legitimacy is guaranteed by their use in mature works of Bach. (1) Subject and answer may not be in exact alternation. See, e.g. I 1, where the order is S.A.A.S, or I 12, where it is S.A.S.S.[59] (2) The entries may overlap one another, that is, one may begin before the previous one is finished. This procedure is known as *stretto,* and may be applied as between any two or more voices. Perhaps the classic example is the chorus 'Gratias agimus tibi' from Bach's *Mass in B minor* (ex. 22).

[59] Or the chorus 'His yoke is easy' from Handel's *Messiah,* which is still a fugue although all four voices enter in the same key.

Ex. 22

The 'Confiteor' from the same work is a superb case in *five* parts, with the addition of an independent running-bass. See also the chorus 'And I will exalt Him' from Handel's *Israel in Egypt,* and the '48', I 19.

This feature may be combined with another—melodic inversion of the subject or answer as in II 3 (ex. 23).

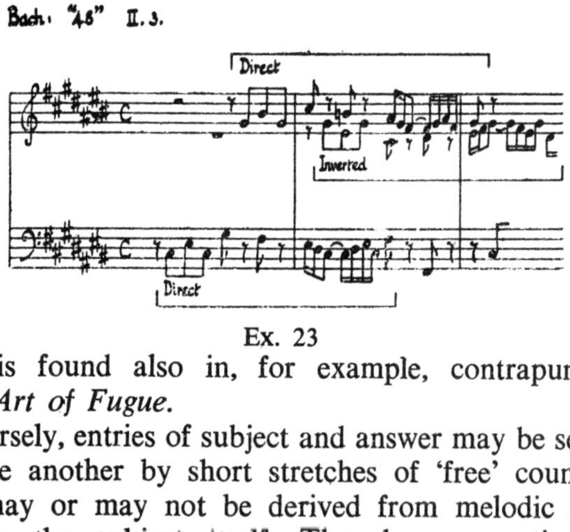

Ex. 23

This is found also in, for example, contrapunctus V of *The Art of Fugue.*

Conversely, entries of subject and answer may be separated from one another by short stretches of 'free' counterpoint which may or may not be derived from melodic material found in the subject itself. Though comparatively rare between the *first* statements of subject and answer (I 7), it is a commonplace in the later part of the exposition, and needs no particular illustration. For examples taken at random see I 2, bars 5-6; I 12 bars 10-12; II 12, bars 8-11. These 'free' bars are usually known as 'codettas'.

Countersubject. When the second voice begins to give the answer the opening voice may do one of two things: either it can continue in free counterpoint with the answer, with no object other than to provide a satisfactory partnership with it; or it can proceed to give out a *countersubject.* The latter can be recognised only by reference to later stages of the fugue, where it will be found in company with the subject at all (or at any rate most) of its appearances. The essentials of a countersubject are that it shall be in *double counterpoint* with the subject (i.e. it must be capable of being played either as a treble or a bass to the latter), and that it shall be well contrasted with it in rhythm and/or melody, so that both can be easily recognised when played simultaneously (ex. 24).

Bach: "48" II. 15, bar 4.

Ex. 24a

Ibid, bar 54

Ex. 24b

Examples of first-class countersubjects may be seen in I 7 and I 16.

Some fugues have two countersubjects; the second of these is introduced by the first voice when the third voice takes up the subject, while the second voice proceeds with the first countersubject; and so on, the three melodies being in triple counterpoint so that any of the three can be bass to the others. The variety of effect, coupled with economy of means, obtainable from the several combinations of the themes, made this a favourite method with Bach, whose works provide many examples of fugues of sturdy build, the main structural supports of which are well-spaced entries of the three themes in different positions and in different keys. See, for example, I 21:

The treble voice has the subject first. When the middle voice answers, the treble has the 1st counter-subject; when the bass enters (bar 9) the middle voice has the 1st countersubject, and the treble the 2nd countersubject. We have a piece of triple counterpoint which may be diagrammatically described thus:

CS 2
CS 1
S

Thereafter we find the following positions of the three themes:

bar 13	S CS2; CS1	bars 22 and 41	CS1 S, CS2	bar 26	CS2 CS1; S	bar 37	S CS1 CS2

Observe that Bach does not use all the possible positions of the themes, but that he does use two of them twice. It is characteristic of him that he rarely exhausted the possibilities of his multiple counterpoint, preferring perfection of total design to the boring process of hammering home points which, if not used with restraint, tend merely to become exhibitions of pedantry.

Other fugues of the '48' having two counter-subjects are I 2 and I 3.

There is, of course, no theoretical limit to the number of counter-subjects which may appear in a fugue, though it is very rare indeed to find more than two. I 12 is an isolated example of a subject and three counter-subjects in quadruple counterpoint, only two of the possible 24 positions being actually shown.

It should now be apparent to the student that the exposition of a fugue offers scope for an almost endless variety of effect. Before analysing a few examples as models, there remain two matters for mention. The first is the *redundant entry,* an additional entry (usually in the original opening voice) in the alternating tonic-dominant sequence, before the exposition ends. It has been remarked that a counter-subject must be in double counterpoint with the subject. Now, it will be clear that in fugues where the opening entries are made by the voices in order of pitch from highest to lowest or vice versa, the counter-subject will have been heard only above the subject, or only below it (as the case may be) at the point where all voices have given the subject once. The first voice therefore has a redundant entry while the last voice has the counter-subject, for the purpose of exhibiting the opposite position of the double counterpoint. A diagram will make this clear:

Treble: Subject .. C.-subject .. Free .... Answer (redundant entry)
Alto: .... Answer .... C.-subject .. Free ....
Bass: .... Subject .... C.-subject ....

A fugue which proceeds exactly according to this diagram is I 7, where the redundant entry occurs in the treble at bar 11. I 21 shows a redundant entry of the treble at bar 13.

The other matter requiring mention is the *counter-exposition,* a purely optional feature rarely found except in fugues of substantial dimensions. This is really a second exposition in which the tonic and dominant keys are retained for the entries; the order of entry is altered, those which had the subject now, as a rule, having the answer; and *vice versa.* Counter-expositions may be seen, for example, in I 9, bars 7-10; and II 17, bars 13-24. Counter-expositions often show special features: I 1, II 7 and II 9, for instance, have counter-expositions in which the entries are taken in *stretto.* The last-named manages a complete counter-exposition in this way in the space of 3½ bars, compared with an exposition which took seven. Another special feature is shown in I 15, bars 20-31, where we find a complete counter-exposition of the *inverted* subject. Finally, we must mention that counter-expositions may be incomplete (II 4, II 16). Some theorists prefer to class an incomplete counter-exposition as a number of redundant entries. This is a matter of nomenclature, and does not warrant argument.

Appended are model analyses of four fugue-expositions from the '48' to serve as guide to the student in his own work.

II 1 (3 voices)

Bar 1 Subject in alto, C major.
5 Tonal answer in treble starting *at* and ending *in* the dominant. Alto in free running counterpoint which is an extension and derivation of bars 3-4 of the subject.
9 Subject in bass, tonic key; atlo and treble free.
13 End of exposition.

I 16 (4 voices)

Bar 1 Subject in alto, G minor, containing two melodic figures.
2(½) Tonal answer in dominant, treble; counter-subject in alto, derived from the two figs. of the subject inverted and in reverse order.
4 Codetta of 1 bar, continuing bar 3 upward in two sequential steps.
5 Subject in bass, tonic. Counter-subject in treble. Alto in free counterpoint.
6(½) Answer in tenor, dominant. Counter-subject in bass. Treble in free counterpoint with an imitation of the subject. Alto silent.
8 End of exposition.

I 3 (3 voices)

Bar 1 Subject, C sharp major, treble.
3 Tonal answer in dominant, alto. 1st counter-subject in treble.
5 Subject, tonic, in bass; 1st counter-subject in alto, 2nd counter-subject in treble.
7 Episode modulating almost at once to the dominant and remaining there. The bass develops a semiquaver figure derived by inversion from the 1st counter-subject; the upper parts are in dialogue on a new figure.
10 Redundant entry of answer in dominant in treble voice; 1st counter-subject in alto, showing for the first time *below* the subject. The bass part is free.
12 Full-close in dominant; end of exposition.

I 1 (4 voices)

Bar 1, beat 1 Subject, alto, C major.
Bar 2, beat 3 Real answer, treble, in dominant. Alto free, starting with a continuation of the final figure of the subject.
4, beat 1 Answer (!) in tenor, tonic key but *on* the dominant. The treble is a free inversion of the previous alto part. The alto is free.

5, beat 3	Subject, tonic key, in bass. The other three parts are freely derived from figures of the subject.
7, beat 1	Start of counter-exposition. Subject, treble, tonic.
7, beat 3	Answer on dominant in *stretto,* tenor voice. The bass is free, the alto silent.
9, beat 1	Answer (!), dominant, alto. The other parts free, the bass being silent after three beats.
10, beat 3	Answer, dominant, in bass.
11, beat 1	The alto, in *stretto,* has the subject on the dominant of the dominant, closing the counter-expostion in an unusual way.
12, beat 1	Beginning of development proper.

(b) *The continuation or development of the fugue*

While all fugues must have an exposition, their continuation is a matter in which several differing procedures are possible. Some theorists would divide the continuation into 'middle' and 'final' sections; but this, though frequently possible, is as often as not contrary to the effect upon the ear, which is usually one of continuous expansion and development of the material of the subject and counter-subject(s) through a number of keys, reaching a point at which, with more-or-less climactic effect, a return is made to the home-key. Only in those cases where the composer makes a point of a strong final entry or entries of the subject in the tonic key, or of a recapitulation, is one aware of a tripartite structure, and it is contrary to common sense to insist upon the existence of a 'final section' where there is nothing 'sectional' about the matter.

I 3 (bar 42), I 16 (bar 28), and II 17 (bar 41) are among the fugues in the '48' which may fairly be said to have true 'final sections'. On the other hand there is no point in I 1, I 10 or II 12 (for instance) at which the ear is conscious of the start of any independent final section.

Other fugues, as R. O. Morris has pointed out, are clearly 'open' two-part forms, written exactly on the principles of the movements of the suites. I 6 shows this very plainly, even to the recapitulation at the end, in the tonic key, of the cadential bars 17-21 which closed the first part in the dominant key.

Again, many fugues have a formal extension of the cadence which may fairly be described as a coda, since it sounds like one; but this does not seem to justify the stand taken by some writers, who maintain that everything following the end of the last entry of the subject *must* be classified as such.

When all things are considered, we are driven to the conclusion which instinct probably indicated from the start—that each fugue must be described as it stands, and regarded as an individual composition to be judged on its own merits as music. As in the case of the exposition, however, certain common means of procedure may be discussed and illustrated as an aid to understanding the composer's method of arriving at his result.

It is only logical and artistically fitting that the two keys which formed the basis of the tonality of the exposition should not be conspicuous during the development of the fugue; and in fact, though there are exceptions, the composer, after the exposition, usually writes an 'episode' during which a modulation is made to some related key not so far heard, and in that key an entry or entries of the subject are then made. Thence, by alternation of episodical matter with formal entries, the development is built up, making use of a variety of keys in the process. This relief from the basic tonality of the fugue serves the additional purpose of increasing the sense of structural unity which is achieved when the music ultimately does return to the home-tonic, whether in the form of a 'final section' or not.

Technically, an *episode* is any passage coming after the exposition of a fugue, in which the subject is not actually being sounded. Besides its function as a vehicle for modulation, it offers the composer great scope for thematic development and expansion of figures derived from subject or counter-subject, or even unrelated to them. I 16 has (if we disregard for the present purpose short linking passages of less than one bar's length) two episodes, the first at bars 8-11, the second at bars 24-28. In each of these, one of the middle voices is silent throughout, and makes the more effective entry with the subject subsequently. In each, great play is made of the figure found in bar 2 of the subject, and its inversion as found in the counter-subject. Apart from these points, however, they differ from one another greatly, the first being of a discursive type whose main object is to get to the key of B flat major, while the second develops sequentially, making ordered use of a 4-note figure of no particular thematic significance, in alternation between the upper parts. By contrast with this, the two episodes of I 21 (bars 17-22 and 30-35) are both based upon the same running counterpoint derived from the *end* of the subject, against a freely inverted form of the *beginning* of the subject; differing from one another chiefly in the fact that in the first the running part is the treble, while in the second it is the bass. Close examination of the large number of episodes in I 3 and I 7, which vary greatly in length and scope, is recommended as a means of acquiring quickly some acquaintance with Bach's methods. It may be mentioned in passing that the distinction between *episode* and *codetta* (as these words are used in connection with fugue) is purely arbitrary, those episodes which occur before the end of the exposition being technically styled codettas.[60]

The texture of some fugues is so closely connected with the subject itself as to preclude the use of episodes altogether, or to reduce them to slight linking or modulating passages of a beat or two. Such is the case in the very first fugue of the '48', in which the listener's whole attention must be devoted to the enormous number of entries of the subject in stretto, the display of which is the main object of the fugue. Breathing-spaces such as are afforded by episodes would upset the whole plan, reducing what is an overwhelming effect of accumulation to a boring series of fresh starts.

Having just noticed that I 1 is an example of a fugue

[60] Tovey and Morris in their writings have set the excellent fashion of abolishing this very artificial distinction.

deliberately written to display effects of *stretto*, it seems appropriate now to point out that while stretto is a legitimate device which may be used by a composer at any point in a fugue where it is likely to be artistically effective, or not at all, many fugues do in fact exist whose main musical point lies in their systematic employment of stretto. In the '48' we have, besides that already mentioned, nos. I 8, I 20, I 22, II 5, II 7, II 9 and II 22, to all of which this applies. The staggering case of Contrapunctus V of *The Art of Fugue* must be cited, in which stretto at four different distances, direct and inverted, is displayed with a fantastic ingenuity which does not prevent the fugue from sounding like a smoothly-written piece of counterpoint, even if it is not one of Bach's greatest pieces of music. So also, mention must be made of the chorus 'Gratias agimus tibi' from the *Mass in B minor* (already noticed in a more restricted connection), which presents us with a solid block of stretto on two different subjects, in which at one point (beginning at bar 25) there are actually thirteen entries of the main subject in stretto. And this is no dry exercise in counterpoint, but a piece of music so noble and moving that Bach was constrained to make an absolute exception of it by using its music again at the end of the Mass to the words 'Dona nobis pacem'.

The devices known as 'diminution' (that is, playing the subject in shorter notes) and 'augmentation' (the subject in longer notes) are sometimes used in stretto, as well as in their own right. These two artifices are particularly open to abuse at the hands of composers whose artistry lags behind their ingenuity. It is notable that Bach rarely uses them (though his ability to hold his own with anybody in the matter of ingenuity is amply demonstrated in Contrapunctus VI and VII of *The Art of Fugue*); where he does, apart from such demonstrations, it is always to some musical purpose, as in the playful diminutions of II 3, the increased momentum of the diminutions of II 9, or the impressive climactic effect of the augmentations in I 8, II 2 and II 3.

Of the device known as 'cancrizans', i.e., playing the subject backwards, it is necessary only to say this: that only one example of its being *recognisable* by the ear at all is on record, and that in a fugue which, though a masterpiece, is scarcely likely to be cited as a model for students, viz., the last movement of Beethoven's *'Hammerklavier' sonata (op. 106).*

On the whole it is true to say that the highest artistic point reached in fugue lies not in the employment of inversion, stretto, diminution, augmentation and the like, but in the skilful use of double, triple and quadruple counterpoint, whether or not enhanced by 'devices'. That Bach was of this opinion is shown by his reserving the later part of *The Art of Fugue* for fugues which rely upon these factors for their point.

We have so far mentioned double and multiple counterpoint only in connection with counter-subjects; but there remains for consideration (briefly, for proper treatment would require a whole volume) the subject of double and triple fugue.

I 4 and II 14 are triple fugues on the plan of introducing three subjects one at a time, combining the second with the first in double counterpoint, and then the third with the other two in triple counterpoint. The question of whether the first appearances of the second and third subjects shall be by way of individual expositions or whether they shall from the first be seen in combination with their predecessors is a detail of fugal construction which varies with different works: II 14 shows the former method, I 4 the latter. The glory of these two fugues, and of others such as II 18 (double), *The Art of Fugue* IX and X (double), VIII and XI (triple) lies in the variety of beautiful musical effects obtained from the display of the counterpoint in different positions.

A type of double fugue much favoured by Handel and Mozart, though rare in Bach, introduces two subjects simultaneously. See the 'Kyrie' of Mozart's *Requiem*; 'He smote all the first-born of Egypt' from Handel's *Israel in Egypt*; the last movement of Haydn's string quartet op. 20 no. 5; and no. 32 of Beethoven's *Diabelli variations*. R. O. Morris remarks that there is no example of this type of fugue in the '48', but (surprisingly enough) a good example *is* to be found in the *prelude* of I 7, starting from bar 25.

Before giving analyses of complete fugues to serve as models, we now append notes upon one or two other relevant matters.

A *fughetta* is a short fugue, consisting usually of an exposition and a short conclusion, with little or no development. Certain fugues in the '48' (e.g., I 5, I 9) are so described by Tovey.

Fugato, not to be confused with the above, means 'fugued' and is the term used to describe a passage in a work not otherwise fugal (perhaps the development section of a sonata-form) in which voices are brought in in the manner of a fugal exposition.

Gigue, the dance with which most of Bach's suites and partitas end, is commonly an open 2-part piece consisting of two fughettas, the second on a subject which is the inversion of that of the first. See the gigues of the *French suites nos. 1, 4* and *5*; of the *English suites nos. 3, 5* and *6*; and of the *Partitas nos. 3* and *6.*

Accompanied Fugue. A piece in which the vocal parts are in fugue, with an orchestral accompaniment entirely independent of the themes of the fugue itself.

Fugue on a Chorale. Usually a specialised form of Chorale Prelude, in which, during the course of a fugue based on the tune of the choral, one voice, to which no other part in the music is allotted, gives out the entire chorale-melody, one line at a time, in long notes by way of a *canto fermo.*

We now analyse in detail three fugues of different kinds, both to illustrate Bach's methods and to serve as models for the kind of analysis which will teach the student more than any text-book can; provided, that is, that his analysis is the preliminary to attentive listening to the music.

II 12:

A 3-voice fugue with no clear-cut final section, no countersubject, and none of the 'devices' of fugal construction. The following analysis does no more than show that the structural technique which lies behind the musical effects described on pages 144-5 consists largely of the careful balancing of formal entries of subject and answer with free alternating episodes.

Bar 1 Subject in treble, tonic, ending on the first note of bar 4, and followed by a link of 5 semiquavers.

5 Tonal answer in dominant, in alto; the treble part is free, and begins by imitating bar 3 of the subject.

8 4-bar codetta continuing the contrapuntal style of bar 7.

12 Subject, bass, tonic. The other parts free.

15 Beginning of development. First episode of 10 bars continuing the style and referring at its start to bar 3, and later in alternate bars (17, 19, 21) to the repeated-note figure from bar 1 of the subject. The harmony leads quickly to the key of A flat, on whose dominant the episode ends.

25 Subject, A flat major, treble. Free running counterpoint in bass; alto silent.

29 Answer, E flat major (i.e., dominant of A flat) in alto. Treble and bass free.

32 Second episode of 9 bars. This reproduces the style and main features of episode 1, being in fact in part a transposition thereof with the upper parts reversed. The episode closes with a firm cadence in C minor, which is at once made major and thus the home-dominant.

41 At this point we return to F minor, and some commentators maintain that this is the start of the final section. No feeling of separation from what has gone before exists, however. Subject, F minor, in bass. Upper parts free.

44 Third episode of 7 bars, starting by reproducing 43-44 in free sequence, but containing no significant thematic derivations, and continuing the general style.

51 Subject, tonic key, in alto, the bass on a dominant pedal reiterating the repeated-note figure from bar 1, the treble in free semiquaver counterpoint.

54 Fourth episode of 18 bars. The main point about this episode is that, like the shorter ones, it continues unflaggingly to maintain the momentum and general style of the piece. However, a new feature is the use of the figure of the whole of bar 1 in the bass during the sequential passages at bars 56-58 and 62-64, while bars

66-70 are related to episodes 1 and 2. At the end, the harmony moves in a subdominant direction.

72 Subject, B flat minor, in treble. Other parts free.

75 Subject, tonic, alto. Technically in stretto, though no point is served by insisting on this almost accidental fact. The bass is derived by inversion from bar 4, though again, since so much of the semiquaver counterpoint is related in a general way, the fact is of little significance. More important is the treble which twice insists upon the repeated-note figure, and the general fact that the harmonic basis is quite different from any previous episode.

78 Coda, which has the air of being a 5th episode, being related to the corresponding passages of the 1st, 2nd and 4th episodes, and showing its special position only in its being over a dominant pedal and coming to a strong full close.

II 9:

A very close-knit 4-voice fugue showing stretto, diminution and inversion, and a counter-subject which is irregular to the extent that it does not often appear along with the subject after the end of the exposition. This fugue is a great contrast to II 12.

Bar 1 Subject, bass, tonic key.

2, beat 3 Real answer, tenor, dominant; counter-subject in bass.

4 Subject, alto, tonic. Counter-subject in tenor.

5, beat 3 Answer, treble, dominant. Counter-subject in alto.

7 Codetta of 2 bars; all voices are in vaguely derivative pure counterpoint. At bar 8 the bass holds a dominant pedal ,and the tenor has a modified version of the latter part of the counter-subject.

9 Counter-exposition, in which in 3 bars all the voices enter in stretto in the order A.T.B.S., the first making a new unaccompanied start. Observe (1) that the alto's first note is shortened; (2) that the order of entry is changed so that voices which in the exposition had the subject now have the answer, and *vice versa*; (3) the order is answer, subject, answer, subject; (4) there is no room in this close counterpoint for the counter-subject.

12, beat 3 Episode beginning the development. The sequel shows that this may fairly be called a 'middle section'. There is a sudden switch to the dominant chord of F sharp minor, leading into 3½ bars in which the scale figure from the counter-subject is a promiment feature in all voices. The tonality moves towards C sharp minor.

16-18 A pair of entries of the subject in alto and treble in stretto at one bar's distance, at the fifth above. The pitch of the entries is the original tonic and dominant, but the harmony begins in C sharp minor, moves through E major and approaches B major.

19-21 A similar pair of entries in bass and tenor starting on the dominant and supertonic respectively, harmonised in B major moving to F sharp minor. The tenor entry is rhythmically modified at the end.

22 Episode of 1 bar leading to strong dominant of F sharp minor.

23-24 A pair of entries of the subject, treble and alto, with some slight rhythmic modification, and with the leap of a third filled in. The entries are in stretto at the 4th below, at one beat's distance. The harmony moves towards C sharp minor.

25 A pair of entries modified as were the last pair; bass and tenor at one beat's distance at the 5th above. Key of C sharp minor.

26-29 A series of entries of the subject in diminution, in pairs of stretti thus: treble and alto, tenor and bass. Each pair is at two beat's distance, at the 4th below. The tonality shifts between E major and B major.

30, beat 3 A full entry in the alto at tonic pitch is accompanied by entries in diminution as follows: bar 30 beat 2, bass; bar 30 beat 4, tenor, freely inverted; bar 31 beat 2, treble, inverted; bar 31 beat 4, tenor, inverted.

32, beat 3 Episode of 3 bars derived from the diminished subject, coming to a full close in G sharp minor.

35 Beginning of clearly-defined final section, with a plunge back to the home-tonic.[61] A grand stretto in which the entries of the subject in its normal form are combined with entries in inverted diminution as follows: normal entries, bar 35

[61] Bach is fond of this sudden plunge from the mediant minor straight into the tonic. See *Brandenburg no. 2*, 1st movement, bar 102, etc.

beat 2, alto starting on dominant; bar 35 beat 3, tenor starting on tonic; bar 36 beat 3, bass starting on dominant; bar 37 beat 4, treble starting on tonic. Inverted diminished entries: bar 35 beat 2, treble; bar 36 beat 4, alto; bar 37 beat 4, tenor. Each of the diminished entries runs into a modified version of the counter-subject.

39 An episodical bar continuing the matter of bar 38 downward in sequence. The bass is silent.

40 Subject in bass, starting on the dominant. Counter-subject modified in alto.

41, beat 3 Coda of 2½ bars.

I 8:

A 3-voice stretto-fugue of great complexity, making much use of 'devices'.

Bar 1 Subject, alto, tonic.

3, beat 3 Tonal answer, treble, dominant. The alto is free, there being no counter-subject.

6 Codetta of 2 bars.

8 Subject, bass, tonic.

10, beat 4 Codetta of 1¼ bars.

12 Redundant entry of answer, bass, dominant.

15 Beginning of development; episode of 4½ bars unrelated to subject-matter.

19 beat 3 1st stretto. A pair of entries, alto and treble, in stretto at the half-bar at the octave above, with free bass-part. Key A sharp minor.

23 Episode of 1 bar.

24 2nd stretto. A close stretto at the 5th below, the voices separated from each other by only one beat. The order is treble, alto, bass, the alto being rhythmically modified and the bass incomplete, being really extra to the overall scheme of stretti (as will be seen).

27 3rd stretto, treble and alto at half-bar at the 5th below, with free bass derived from the 3rd-6th notes of the subject. Key C sharp major.

30 Subject inverted in treble, F sharp major.

33 3-bar episode.

36 Subject inverted in alto, D sharp minor.

39 Answer inverted in bass, at dominant of D sharp minor.

41, beat 3 3-bar episode.

44, beat 3 4th stretto, between bass and treble on the inverted subject at the half-bar and octave above, i.e., this stretto corresponds to the first one.

47, beat 3 5th stretto between alto and treble, on the inverted subject at one beat and the 4th above. The treble is modified rhythmically in the same way as the alto at bar 24; i.e., this stretto corresponds to the second one.

50 2-bar episode.

52 6th stretto of all three voices at one beat's distance and at the octave above, on the subject in its direct position. None of the entries is complete.

54 7th stretto of all three voices at one beat's distance and at the octave above, on the inverted subject. None of the entries is complete (i.e., the converse of the 6th stretto).

56 1½-bar episode.

57, beat 3 Subject, treble, tonic key. This might be called the beginning of the final section if there were any musical feeling to back up the appearance in print.

60 1½-bar episode.

61, beat 3 8th stretto. The alto has the subject first; after two beats the bass enters with the subject in augmentation at the 5th below, and its full course allows time for completion of the alto entry and of a treble entry of the inverted subject starting at bar 64, beat 3.

67 9th stretto, similar to the 8th. Here the bass opens with the subject; after two beats the alto has the augmented subject, and at bar 69 beat 3, the treble enters with the subject in normal form.

72, beat 3 Subject, alto.

75 2-bar episode.

77 10th stretto. The bass opens with the subject in the tonic key. At one beat's distance the alto has the rhythmically-expanded version as found at bars 24 and 47, and again at one beat's distance the treble has the subject in full augmentation. All three entries are at the octave above. At bar 80, beat 3, while the treble is in the middle of its augmented entry, the alto has a further full entry in normal form, the harmony leaning very strongly to the subdominant side.

83 Coda of 5 bars.

Fugue since Bach

In its essentials, fugue has not changed since Bach's day. The principles of the fugal method have been applied by composers of such different periods and styles as Mozart, Beethoven, Brahms, Verdi and Vaughan Williams with masterly effect. The fugues of each of these masters, considered as music, sound like *and are* typical examples of their own individual composition. Each of them, in fact, is using for his own purposes a basic common material, and the differing results are a fascinating commentary upon the flexibility, adaptability and inherent soundness of the fugal method.

Analysis of nineteenth and twentieth-century fugue should present no difficulty to the student who has been through a course of study of Bach's work, provided he keeps his ears and eyes open. He will find a greater freedom of action in the matter of episode, a wider range of key, a more dramatic use of key *contrast*, at times a tendency to incorporate non-contrapuntal matter by way of relief, and a heightened sense of drama in the presentation of the subject-matter, especially at climactic points. The last-named feature is partly the natural outcome of the development of the dramatic side of music since Bach's day, and is of course aided by the immense expansion of the resources of musical colour. With a modern orchestra at his disposal, a composer has the means at hand to display the material of his fugue with greater superficial vividness than was the case in Bach's day.

The following are among the very many examples worth the student's attention:

Haydn	Finale of *string quartet in F minor (op. 20 no. 5)*
	'For He both Heaven and earth hath clothed' from *The Creation,* part I
Mozart	'Kyrie' from the *Requiem*
	Fugue in C minor for two pianos (K.426) or for string quartet (K.546).
Beethoven	*Pianoforte sonata in A flat (op. 110)* (finale)
	Symphony no. 9, last movt., bars 655-729.
	Overture, *Consecration of the House* (from bar 89)
Mendelssohn	*Organ Sonata no. 2* (finale)

Brahms	Fugue from the *Variations on a theme of Handel* op. 24
	'Der gerichten Seelen sind in Gottes Hand', from the 3rd movt. of the *German Requiem.*
Rheinberger	Last movements of *Organ Sonatas nos. 3, 4, 13, 15* (etc.).
Liszt	Organ *Fugue on the name B.A.C.H.*
Verdi	'Sanctus' and 'Libera me' from the *Requiem.*
Franck	Fugue from the *Prelude, Chorale and Fugue* for piano.
Bloch	*String quartet no. 2* (last part of finale).
Weinberger	Fugue from *Schwanda the Bagpiper.*
Britten	Fugue from *The Young Person's Guide to the Orchestra.*

2. *Canon*

Canon (the name is a contraction of 'fuga per canonem,' literally 'fugue according to the strict rule') is, like fugue, not a form but a contrapuntal method; *a* canon being a piece of music entirely written *in* canon. It does not offer the same scope as fugue, owing to the severe limitations imposed by the 'strict rule', which ordains that each participating voice, once launched, must imitate diatonically the exact movements of the leader from start to finish, with the slightly humanising concession that modulation may be brought about by the altering of intervals by means of accidentals in the 'following' parts. There may, of course, be any distance and interval between voices that the composer chooses, and the 'following' voices may be direct or inverted imitations, and may be diminished or augmented; though the use of the latter devices in canon is likely to lead to results of the most barren description.

A canon '2 in 1' is one in which two voices participate, both having the same melody. Likewise, the descriptions '3 in 1', '4 in 1' and so on, refer in the first instance to the number of voices, and in the second to the number of melodies being played or sung. More complex and ingenious forms are to be found when several parts sing more than one melody in more than one canon simultaneously; thus, canon '4 in 2' or '6 in 3' refer to pieces in which 4 and 6 voices sing respectively 2 and 3 simultaneous canons.

Such pieces tend to be very artificial, and instances of their musical use are virtually confined to small items such as single variations in sets, and so on. The following instances, if scrutinised with care, will suffice to let the student understand the possibilities of various types of canon:

2 in 1 at the octave below	Beethoven, no. 22 of the *32 variations in C minor.*
2 in 1 at the 9th above	Bach, no. 27 of the *'Goldberg' variations.*
2 in 1 by inversion at the octave	Brahms, second part of no. 6 of the *Variations on a theme of Handel* (The first part is direct canon at the octave below.)
2 in 1 by inversion and augmentation	Bach, the first of the canons in *The Art of Fugue.*

Those who are interested in the more complex types of canon will find excellent examples at the end of Ouseley's *Counterpoint, Canon and Fugue.*

The 'round' is a form of social musical entertainment in the form of an endless canon at the unison, each part entering at a fixed interval of time after its predecessor. Such are 'Three Blind Mice', 'Frère Jacques,' 'London's Burning,' etc. Beethoven was fond of applying the 'round' principle in unexpected places, such as the coda of the finale of the *9th symphony.*

The 'catch' is a round whose words are so arranged as to convey a double or equivocal meaning when sung; they were favourites with the eighteenth-century 'Anacreontic Societies' and other convivial gatherings. The music of many catches by Purcell is printed in the 'Purcell Society' edition, but as the words can only be found by research in the British Museum or similar libraries, the point of them is largely lost.

Probably the most valuable canons are those in which the two parts in canon are accompanied by a third part in free counterpoint. The musical stiffness which characterises almost every canon which is not thus freed from complete slavery to the exigencies of the 'strict rule' can be eliminated by means of the harmonic subtleties which the free part is at liberty to introduce. The best examples to be found are those already mentioned (page 129) from Bach's *'Goldberg' Variations,* giving one at every interval from the unison to the octave, at a diversity of distances. Two of these (variations 12 and 15) are by contrary motion.

On the whole, however, canon is most useful as a device for occasional use during the course of longer compositions. Examples of canon used thus are common in the works of the classical composers and others. The following are a few examples:

Bach	'Et in unum dominum' from the *Mass in B minor.* Bars 19-26.
Mozart	*Piano sonata in D (K.576)* 1st movt. Bars. 28-33.
Beethoven	*Symphony no. 4,* 1st movt., bars 141-157.
Mozart	*Sonata in E minor for violin and piano (K.304)* 1st movt., bars 77-84.
Franck	*Symphony in D minor,* 1st movt., at the 'Lento' just before letter 'O'.
	Ibid., last movt., between letters 'G' and 'H'.
	Sonata for violin and pianoforte, last movt., opening.
Sibelius	*Sonatina (no. 2) in E for pianoforte* (1st movt., bars 1-17).

X

CONCLUSION

As explained in the first chapter, this book does not include in its scope any attempt at full discussion of post-classical developments in the structural aspect of music. It will be well, however, to devote a brief space to an outline of some of the main lines upon which composers have worked during the last century or so.

The early romantic composers such as Schumann and Liszt indubitably felt that the sonata form, as illustrated in the works of Mozart and Beethoven, was in the nature of a set of fetters upon the imagination. This feeling was none the less genuine for being a product of romanticism itself; the romantics were in their day the progressives, and though we can now see that their outlook was of their day, and not for all time, it is necessary to take note of its results in a vast body of important music covering nearly a century.

Two main lines of development follow from their dissatisfaction with the so-called trammels of the sonata form. The first is to be found in the attempts of composers such as Berlioz, Tchaikovsky, Dvořák, Franck and Elgar to bring greater 'unity' to the sonata form by providing thematic links between movements. To the romantic composer, the æsthetic significance of a series of structurally perfect movements related to one another only by emotional considerations was not great; and several methods were employed, not always with artistic success, to achieve greater 'coherence' by the transference of thematic material from one movement to another. Tchaikovsky's 4th and 5th symphonies and Berlioz's 'Symphonie Fantastique' are examples of works in which a dramatic 'motto theme' intrudes upon the internal organisation of the various movements, sometimes in a rhythmical transformation. Again, we have the case of Dvorák's *5th symphony,* in whose last movement is found development of material from all four movements, reaching a climax in the fortissimo statement of the chords which provided a quiet atmospheric opening to the *second* movement, and whose original purpose was to modulate between the keys of the first two movements. Not everybody feels that the æsthetic value of such a process equals its ingenuity. Similarly, the finale of César Franck's *Symphony* makes extensive use of material from the two other movements. In Elgar's *Symphony no. 1,* in addition to a last-movement return to the main theme of the first movement, we find the theme of the scherzo used, in a rhythmic transformation, as the chief melody of the slow movement.

Such methods are not to be confused with the introduction of momentary references to earlier movements in the finale of Beethoven's *9th symphony,* which is not intended to introduce any element of 'structural unity' as between movements.

The effectiveness and point of such interchanges of material vary very much with individual circumstances, and in making estimates of their value, each case must be taken on its merits. The delightful effect, in Brahms's 3rd symphony and in Elgar's 2nd, of the final references to the openings of the works, is in large part due to their unpretentiousness; they perform a function in closing the work with a unifying glance back at the beginning, whose significance is æsthetic and not merely intellectual. As much cannot be said for certain other examples.

Still more root-and-branch efforts at 'unifying' the sonata form may be seen in such works as Liszt's pianoforte sonata in B minor, where an attempt is made to cast all the movements of a normal sonata into one vast 'sonata form'.

It is significant, perhaps, that more recent composers like Sibelius and Vaughan Williams have made a return to the classic line of approach to the symphony, albeit in a manner adapted to the type of rhythmic, melodic and harmonic material with which they work.

The second method adopted by the 'high romantics' to replace the 'outmoded' classical forms was more thoroughly revolutionary, and was first apparent in Liszt's symphonic poems. Here, the music sets out to depict or describe some external story, poem or picture, and is consequently to some extent governed as to its shape by the structure of its 'programme'. Unity is given by the employment of 'motto themes' to which special significance is attached as representing persons, situations, moods or ideas. Such 'motives' are transformed and transmuted in accordance with the different situations which the music is supposed to be describing. Few of such pieces can be said to be thoroughly satisfactory, if only because a detailed description of the 'programme' must be provided before the listener can fully comprehend the composer's intention. Liszt's dozen or so symphonic poems and symphonies include musical portrayals of Hamlet, Orpheus and Faust. Later composers who have made a success of the symphonic poem include Richard Strauss *(Don Juan, Don Quixote, Till Eulenspiegel),* Tchaikovsky *(Romeo and Juliet),* Dukas *(The Sorcerer's Apprentice)* and Elgar *(Falstaff).* Not all Strauss's symphonic poems are so successful as those mentioned above, his attempts at more philosophical subjects *(Also sprach Zarathustra, Tod und Verklärung, Ein Heldenleben)* being uneven in quality, as though the subjects were not entirely suitable for expression in terms of music.

A more satisfying development of the romantic attitude is seen in the 'tone poem', a piece of expressive music designed rather to capture a generalised atmosphere or mood than to depict pictorial detail. Into this class come many of the overtures to romantic operas *(Die Meistersinger, Tannhäuser, Euryanthe)* as well as hundreds of pieces such as Sibelius's *Tapiola* and *En Saga,* Holst's *Egdon Heath,* Delius's *Paris,* and Elgar's *Cockaigne.* The form of such pieces is a matter dependent entirely upon individual circumstances, and is satisfactory if it meets the needs of these circumstances.

The search for suitable forms in which to express the

ever-changing and developing ideas of creative musicians proceeds without ceasing, as it has done since the beginning of music as we know it. Conscious attempts to put the clock back by trying to write modern music in ancient forms, while they may result in occasional *tours de force* like Vaughan Williams's *Mass in G minor,* can never succeed in producing substantial results; this book has missed its target if it has not made it clear that throughout history, changing musical styles have found the forms which met their own requirements. No more is it possible to reach a satisfactory musical structure by conscious and deliberate planning on 'original' lines, and then writing music to fit the plan. Where form and content fit one another exactly, as in Palestrina's *Missa Papae Marcelli,* Purcell's *Dido and Aeneas,* Bach's *Brandenburg Concertos* and *Mass in B minor,* Mozart's 'Jupiter' symphony, Beethoven's *String Quartet in C sharp minor,* Wagner's *Meistersinger* or one of Debussy's piano pieces, you have what may be an imperishable masterpiece. Where they are at odds, the strain will tell sooner or later.

That is the only statement about musical design that can safely be given the status of a dogma.

SHORT BIBLIOGRAPHY

Grove's Dictionary of Music and Musicians
The Oxford Companion to Music (Percy Scholes)

Tovey — *Essays in Musical Analysis* (7 volumes, O.U.P.)
Beethoven (O.U.P.)
Musical Articles from the Encyclopædia Britannica (O.U.P.)
A companion to 'The Art of Fugue' (O.U.P.)
A companion to Beethoven's Pianoforte sonatas (Associated Board)
Notes to individual pianoforte sonatas of Beethoven, and to individual preludes and fugues of the '48' in the Associated Board edition of these works.

Bukofzer — *Music in the Baroque Era* (Dent)

Einstein — *Music in the Romantic Era* (Dent)

Hadow — *Outlines of Musical Form* (from vol. 2 of *Studies in Modern Music* (Seeley)

Hutchings — *A companion to Mozart's Pianoforte Concertos* (O.U.P.)

Morris — *The Structure of Music* (O.U.P.)

Parry — *Style in Musical Art* (Macmillan)

Prout — *Fugue* (Augener)
Musical Form (Augener)
Applied Forms (Augener)

Raymar — Notes to individual pianoforte sonatas of Mozart in the Associated Board edition.

Veinus — *The Concerto* (Cassell)

GLOSSARY

Allemande	The first of the four obligatory dances of the Suite as standardised by Bach.
Anglaise	An indefinite term, used by Bach to describe one of the dances in his 3rd French Suite.
Anglican Chant	A formalised descendant of the Gregorian Chant, being a short harmonised melody to which verses of variable length (usually of the psalms) are sung.
Anthem	The Anglican equivalent of the Motet; early anthems were simply motets sung to English words. The modern use of the word has extended its meaning to any piece of miscellaneous music suitable for singing during a church service.
Arietta	A short aria; by transference, a simple instrumental piece. The most famous instance is the finale of Beethoven's piano sonata, op. 111, an arietta with variations.
Arioso	A cross between pure 'recitative' and pure 'aria', in which the dialogue or action of opera, cantata or oratorio may be carried forward in a more musical and melodious way than by the former. It is especially a feature of 17-century French opera, by contrast with its Italian contemporary.
Bagatelle	A short instrumental piece. The best-known examples are by Beethoven, for piano; they include some very fine examples of his 'late' style.
Ballade	An instrumental piece based upon or inspired by, a poetical 'ballad'.
Ballad Opera	A purely English type of stage entertainment, the dialogue being spoken, and frequently interrupted by songs of a folk- or popular type. The first and greatest was 'The Beggar's Opera' of 1729.
Ballet	1. An English 16th-century part-song, less contrapuntal in texture and more highly rhythmical than the madrigal, usually having a 'Fa la la' refrain. 2. A stage entertainment in which the dance and the music share the honours. Much music written for the ballet is good enough to stand alone as material for

concert-programmes; conversely, the custom has grown up of 'interpreting' music written for the concert-hall in dance on the stage.

Barcarolle A song, and by analogy an instrumental piece, derived from the 'boat-songs' of the Venetian gondoliers.

Beggar's Opera The first and greatest of the 'Ballad Operas', written by John Gay and produced in London in 1729. One of Gay's motives was to ridicule the conventions of the contemporary Italian Opera, and his success in this respect came near to ruining Handel.

Berceuse A lullaby or cradle-song, used by analogy for instrumental pieces of a soothing, deliberately monotonous type.

Bourrée A lively dance found in many 17th-18th century suites.

Bridge-passage Another name for the 'transition' of a sonata form.

Burlesca An instrumental piece of a lively and humorous kind.

Cantata Originally no more than a piece of accompanied vocal music (usually for one singer). The cantata developed both in the sacred and the secular spheres into a substantial composition for soloists, orchestra and choir, with alternating recitative, aria and chorus. The greatest are the 200-odd of J. S. Bach, almost all sacred.

Canticle A hymn used in the services of many branches of the Christian Church. The term now covers the Te Deum, Benedictus, Benedicite, Venite, Jubilate, Cantate Domino, Magnificat and Nunc Dimittis.

Cantiones Sacrae Another name for the motets of the 16th century.

Canto Fermo A melody sung in long notes, round which other parts weave counterpoint, the latter being often derived from the melody of the canto fermo. It is a feature of many masses and motets of the 'Golden Age', particularly in its earlier stages.

Canzonet A madrigal, usually of rather a light type.

Capriccio A short instrumental piece of undefined form, the composer being free to follow his fancy in this respect.

Carol A religious folk-song applicable to a specific season of the Christian Year; invariably joyful.

Cassation A divertimento.

Cavatina A short aria. By transference, a short instrumental piece.

Chamber Music Music designed to be played in a small room, in which each instrumental part is the responsibility of one individual. The term strictly should include solo instrumental music, but is generally understood to apply to from two to nine players. Where more than two players are concerned, the title of the music is generally taken from the instrumental combination which plays it: thus, 'pianoforte trio', 'string quartet', 'wind quintet', etc., all being normally sonatas, in fact if not in name.

Chanson	An early French type of madrigal, for voices alone or for single voice with an instrument. Akin to the 'Airs' of Dowland and other English composers.
Chorale	The English version of the German word 'Choral-Gesang', a hymn-tune of the Lutheran Church.
Chorale-prelude	A piece of organ-music based upon the melody of a chorale. Those of Bach transcend all others in variety and spiritual depth, as well as in technical skill.
Comic opera	Means just what it says. Not to be confused with 'Opera Comique' q.v.
Concert-stück	A single-movement piece for a soloist with orchestra.
Courante	The second of the four obligatory dances of the suite as standardised by Bach.
Cyclic form	Now applied normally to sonata forms in which there is transference of themes from one movement to another.
Diverti-mento	A composition for any collection of instruments, in several movements of a light nature, designed for amusement rather than for intellectual enjoyment. Those of Mozart are the best-known.
Divisions	Early variations on the *double* principle.
Dramma per musica	A term used by the earliest opera composers to describe their compositions.
Ecossaise	A French dance with no traceable connection with Scotland.
Equale	A short funeral piece for trombones. The name is widely known through Beethoven's having written a magnificent set of three.
Etude	A pianoforte piece designed to exploit some particular aspect of technique.
Fantasia	A piece of music in which structural considerations are secondary to the momentary whim of the composer—often exemplifying characteristics which would be regarded as undesirable in good extemporising.
Free Fantasia	Another name for the development section of a sonata form.

Frottola An Italian secular vocal form similar to the French Chanson or the English Ballet.

Galanteries The optional dances of the suite as standardised by Bach, coming as a rule between the Sarabande and the Gigue. They include minuets, gavottes, bourrées, etc.

Galliard A sixteenth-century English dance usually coupled with the slower Pavan.

Gavotte A lively eighteenth-century dance, whose particular rhythmic characteristic is that its phrases all begin on the weak beat of a 2/2 bar. Gavottes appear among the galanteries of many eighteenth-century suites.

Gigue The fourth and last of the obligatory dances of the suite as standardised by Bach.

Glee A peculiarly English vocal form, usually for unaccompanied male voices. Its high period was the late eighteenth-century when it formed the main ingredient of the programmes of the 'Anacreontic Societies' etc. Its peculiarity includes also an almost complete absence of counterpoint.

Grand Opera A technical term meaning an opera in which every word is sung; i.e. there is no spoken dialogue.

Gregorian Chant Plainsong music in which much of the Roman Catholic liturgy is conducted.

Impromptu An instrumental piece supposed to have a somewhat 'free' or 'extempore' character.

Impro-visation An extempore performance in which the acts of composition and execution take place simultaneously. It used to be practised by organists.

Incidental music Music written for performance during the action of a stage play.

Interlude Music of minor importance played between musical or other items of greater significance.

Intermezzo 1. An interlude.
2. An instrumental piece for which there is no other obvious title.

Invention A short instrumental piece.

Leitmotif A theme used in the Wagnerian music-drama in association with a particular person, thing, state of mind, etc., and capable of rhythmic transformation and of combination with other leitmotifs for the conveyance of subtleties of meaning for which words would be too crude a means of expression.

Lesson Another name for suite in the eighteenth-century sense.

Libretto The verbal text of an opera, oratorio, etc.

Lied	A song for voice and pianoforte which attempts to fuse words and music into an inseparable unity.
Light opera	The words mean what they say (cf. Grand opera, comic opera, opera comique).
Loure	A slow dance; one of the galanteries (q.v.).
Madrigal	A secular contrapuntal unaccompanied vocal composition whose heydey was the sixteenth century, when it flourished particularly in Italy and England.
Masque	A lavish and spectacular entertainment carried through by music and action based on a poetical plot; it flourished particularly in the early seventeenth century, but has been revived in a modified sense as a branch of the art of ballet, as for example in Vaughan Williams' 'Job'.
Mass	The central part of the Roman Catholic liturgy. Those parts (the 'Ordinary') which do not vary from day to day are the Kyrie, Gloria, Credo, Sanctus, Benedictus and Agnus Dei, and it is the permanent settings of these by countless composers which are usually referred to when musicians speak of the Mass.
Mazurka	A dance of Polish origin made internationally famous by Chopin's numerous examples.
Melodrama	A composition for speaking voice with instrumental accompaniment.
Minuet	A stately eighteenth-century dance in triple time. One of the galanteries (q.v.).
Monody	Music in which one melodic line transcends the rest of the texture in importance, as opposed to 'polyphony', where all lines are of equal importance. Usually used in connection with the works of the early seventeenth century Italian opera-composers, who are often known as the 'monodists'.
Nocturne	A title popularised by Chopin, for a piece of music, undefined as to form, which claims to capture or suggest the atmosphere of the night (in its more romantic moods).
Nuove musiche	A term used by the Italian opera-composers of the early seventeenth century to distinguish their 'modern' style from the 'antiquated' style of Palestrina.
Opera	A stage entertainment in which music is predominant; that is, the characters of the opera themselves carry forward the play in song.
Opera comique	A technical term used in France to define opera in which the dialogue is spoken, not sung, be the subject comic or otherwise.

Oratorio A large-scale sacred composition employing solo-singers, chorus, and orchestra, usually semi-dramatic in form. Among its origins was the need to provide the public with an alternative to opera during the season of Lent, when stage-performances were forbidden.

Overture The prelude to an important piece of music such as an opera; loose usage has transferred the word also to various independent orchestral pieces, sometimes known as 'concert-overtures'.

Part-song A composition for choir, of the length and scope of a solo-song. Part-songs may be accompanied or not by instruments, at the composer's discretion.

Passepied A quick dance. One of the galanteries (q.v.).

Pastorale An instrumental composition which conveys something of the atmosphere of the countryside, being usually in 6/8 or 12/8 time and over a static bass.

Pavan(e) A slow sixteenth/seventeenth-century English dance, usually coupled with the Galliard.

Polonaise A Polish national dance popularised by Chopin's examples for pianoforte solo.

Postlude A piece played at the end of the Church Service; a 'concluding voluntary'.

Preambule A term used by Bach occasionally as a substitute for 'prelude'.

Prelude Something played before the main business, as the overture to an opera, or the piece preceding a fugue, as in Bach's '48'. The fact that no rules are laid down as to form or design led to its use, by transference, as a generalised name for small instrumental pieces, such as Chopin's preludes.

Programme music Music which claims to illustrate some external story or picture; i.e. music written to a 'programme'.

Quodlibet A piece of music made up by mixing several tunes together, usually with a humorous intention.

Recitative Music in which the inflexions of speech are formalised and given definite pitch; it may be quite free in rhythm, or the composer may attempt to define the relative and absolute lengths of time to be taken by each syllable. The dialogue of opera and oratorio is perforce in recitative of a more or less formal kind.

Requiem A special form of the Mass, for the dead.

Rhapsody The description of the term 'fantasia' will apply here also.

Sarabande The third of the obligatory dances of the suite as standardised by Bach.

Scherzo	Literally, 'a joke'. A quick piece of music usually found as an alternative to the 'minuet' in a sonata, from which it developed by the simple process of speeding up the tempo.
Serenade	1. Another name for 'divertimento'. 2. A song sung by a lover at his lady's window.
Serenata	1. Same as 'serenade' (1). 2. A secular cantata of a pastoral type.
Service	A complete setting of the canticles for use in the Anglican church.
Shanty	A song formerly sung by sailors for the synchronising of communal movements such as capstan-winding. etc.
Siciliano	An old dance in 6/8 or 12/8 time, much used in the eighteenth century for the slow movements of sonatas, etc.
Singspiel	The German equivalent of Ballad Opera (q.v.).
Sonatina	A small sonata.
Song cycle	A series of songs of the 'lied' type, having a connecting link of continuous thought and musically so constructed as to be capable of performance as a whole.
Song form	A name for simple 3-part form, whether 'open' or 'closed'.
Stabat mater	A part of the Roman Catholic liturgy for certain days of the year, frequently set by composers of the 'Golden Age', Palestrina's being at once the best-known and one of his finest works.
Suite	A series of short pieces designed to be played consecutively. In Bach's time it consisted chiefly of dances. *See* Allemande, Courante, Sarabande, Gigue, Galanteries.
Terzetto	A short piece of music for three singers.
Toccata	A fantasia-like solo instrumental piece in which as a rule there occur opportunities for bravura-playing and technical display.
Valse	A nineteenth-century ballroom dance raised to the level of an art-form by Chopin.
Voluntary	Nowadays, a piece of music played by the organist during the assembly or departure of the congregation. (For its somewhat complex history, see 'The Oxford Companion to Music').

A CATALOGUE OF SELECTED DOVER BOOKS
IN ALL FIELDS OF INTEREST

A CATALOGUE OF SELECTED DOVER BOOKS IN ALL FIELDS OF INTEREST

AMERICA'S OLD MASTERS, James T. Flexner. Four men emerged unexpectedly from provincial 18th century America to leadership in European art: Benjamin West, J. S. Copley, C. R. Peale, Gilbert Stuart. Brilliant coverage of lives and contributions. Revised, 1967 edition. 69 plates. 365pp. of text.
21806-6 Paperbound $2.75

FIRST FLOWERS OF OUR WILDERNESS: AMERICAN PAINTING, THE COLONIAL PERIOD, James T. Flexner. Painters, and regional painting traditions from earliest Colonial times up to the emergence of Copley, West and Peale Sr., Foster, Gustavus Hesselius, Feke, John Smibert and many anonymous painters in the primitive manner. Engaging presentation, with 162 illustrations. xxii + 368pp.
22180-6 Paperbound $3.50

THE LIGHT OF DISTANT SKIES: AMERICAN PAINTING, 1760-1835, James T. Flexner. The great generation of early American painters goes to Europe to learn and to teach: West, Copley, Gilbert Stuart and others. Allston, Trumbull, Morse; also contemporary American painters—primitives, derivatives, academics—who remained in America. 102 illustrations. xiii + 306pp. 22179-2 Paperbound $3.00

A HISTORY OF THE RISE AND PROGRESS OF THE ARTS OF DESIGN IN THE UNITED STATES, William Dunlap. Much the richest mine of information on early American painters, sculptors, architects, engravers, miniaturists, etc. The only source of information for scores of artists, the major primary source for many others. Unabridged reprint of rare original 1834 edition, with new introduction by James T. Flexner, and 394 new illustrations. Edited by Rita Weiss. 6⅝ x 9⅝.
21695-0, 21696-9, 21697-7 Three volumes, Paperbound $13.50

EPOCHS OF CHINESE AND JAPANESE ART, Ernest F. Fenollosa. From primitive Chinese art to the 20th century, thorough history, explanation of every important art period and form, including Japanese woodcuts; main stress on China and Japan, but Tibet, Korea also included. Still unexcelled for its detailed, rich coverage of cultural background, aesthetic elements, diffusion studies, particularly of the historical period. 2nd, 1913 edition. 242 illustrations. lii + 439pp. of text.
20364-6, 20365-4 Two volumes, Paperbound $5.00

THE GENTLE ART OF MAKING ENEMIES, James A. M. Whistler. Greatest wit of his day deflates Oscar Wilde, Ruskin, Swinburne; strikes back at inane critics, exhibitions, art journalism; aesthetics of impressionist revolution in most striking form. Highly readable classic by great painter. Reproduction of edition designed by Whistler. Introduction by Alfred Werner. xxxvi + 334pp.
21875-9 Paperbound $2.25

AMERICAN FOOD AND GAME FISHES, David S. Jordan and Barton W. Evermann. Definitive source of information, detailed and accurate enough to enable the sportsman and nature lover to identify conclusively some 1,000 species and sub-species of North American fish, sought for food or sport. Coverage of range, physiology, habits, life history, food value. Best methods of capture, interest to the angler, advice on bait, fly-fishing, etc. 338 drawings and photographs. l + 574pp. $6\frac{5}{8}$ x $9\frac{3}{8}$.
22383-1 Paperbound $4.50

THE FROG BOOK, Mary C. Dickerson. Complete with extensive finding keys, over 300 photographs, and an introduction to the general biology of frogs and toads, this is the classic non-technical study of Northeastern and Central species. 58 species; 290 photographs and 16 color plates. xvii + 253pp.
21973-9 Paperbound $4.00

THE MOTH BOOK: A GUIDE TO THE MOTHS OF NORTH AMERICA, William J. Holland. Classical study, eagerly sought after and used for the past 60 years. Clear identification manual to more than 2,000 different moths, largest manual in existence. General information about moths, capturing, mounting, classifying, etc., followed by species by species descriptions. 263 illustrations plus 48 color plates show almost every species, full size. 1968 edition, preface, nomenclature changes by A. E. Brower. xxiv + 479pp. of text. $6\frac{1}{2}$ x $9\frac{1}{4}$.
21948-8 Paperbound $5.00

THE SEA-BEACH AT EBB-TIDE, Augusta Foote Arnold. Interested amateur can identify hundreds of marine plants and animals on coasts of North America; marine algae; seaweeds; squids; hermit crabs; horse shoe crabs; shrimps; corals; sea anemones; etc. Species descriptions cover: structure; food; reproductive cycle; size; shape; color; habitat; etc. Over 600 drawings. 85 plates. xii + 490pp.
21949-6 Paperbound $3.50

COMMON BIRD SONGS, Donald J. Borror. $33\frac{1}{3}$ 12-inch record presents songs of 60 important birds of the eastern United States. A thorough, serious record which provides several examples for each bird, showing different types of song, individual variations, etc. Inestimable identification aid for birdwatcher. 32-page booklet gives text about birds and songs, with illustration for each bird.
21829-5 Record, book, album. Monaural. $2.75

FADS AND FALLACIES IN THE NAME OF SCIENCE, Martin Gardner. Fair, witty appraisal of cranks and quacks of science: Atlantis, Lemuria, hollow earth, flat earth, Velikovsky, orgone energy, Dianetics, flying saucers, Bridey Murphy, food fads, medical fads, perpetual motion, etc. Formerly "In the Name of Science." x + 363pp.
20394-8 Paperbound $2.00

HOAXES, Curtis D. MacDougall. Exhaustive, unbelievably rich account of great hoaxes: Locke's moon hoax, Shakespearean forgeries, sea serpents, Loch Ness monster, Cardiff giant, John Wilkes Booth's mummy, Disumbrationist school of art, dozens more; also journalism, psychology of hoaxing. 54 illustrations. xi + 338pp.
20465-0 Paperbound $2.75

A HISTORY OF COSTUME, Carl Köhler. Definitive history, based on surviving pieces of clothing primarily, and paintings, statues, etc. secondarily. Highly readable text, supplemented by 594 illustrations of costumes of the ancient Mediterranean peoples, Greece and Rome, the Teutonic prehistoric period; costumes of the Middle Ages, Renaissance, Baroque, 18th and 19th centuries. Clear, measured patterns are provided for many clothing articles. Approach is practical throughout. Enlarged by Emma von Sichart. 464pp. 21030-8 Paperbound $3.00

ORIENTAL RUGS, ANTIQUE AND MODERN, Walter A. Hawley. A complete and authoritative treatise on the Oriental rug—where they are made, by whom and how, designs and symbols, characteristics in detail of the six major groups, how to distinguish them and how to buy them. Detailed technical data is provided on periods, weaves, warps, wefts, textures, sides, ends and knots, although no technical background is required for an understanding. 11 color plates, 80 halftones, 4 maps. vi + 320pp. 6⅛ x 9⅛. 22366-3 Paperbound $5.00

TEN BOOKS ON ARCHITECTURE, Vitruvius. By any standards the most important book on architecture ever written. Early Roman discussion of aesthetics of building, construction methods, orders, sites, and every other aspect of architecture has inspired, instructed architecture for about 2,000 years. Stands behind Palladio, Michelangelo, Bramante, Wren, countless others. Definitive Morris H. Morgan translation. 68 illustrations. xii + 331pp. 20645-9 Paperbound $2.50

THE FOUR BOOKS OF ARCHITECTURE, Andrea Palladio. Translated into every major Western European language in the two centuries following its publication in 1570, this has been one of the most influential books in the history of architecture. Complete reprint of the 1738 Isaac Ware edition. New introduction by Adolf Placzek, Columbia Univ. 216 plates. xxii + 110pp. of text. 9½ x 12¾. 21308-0 Clothbound $10.00

STICKS AND STONES: A STUDY OF AMERICAN ARCHITECTURE AND CIVILIZATION, Lewis Mumford.One of the great classics of American cultural history. American architecture from the medieval-inspired earliest forms to the early 20th century; evolution of structure and style, and reciprocal influences on environment. 21 photographic illustrations. 238pp. 20202-X Paperbound $2.00

THE AMERICAN BUILDER'S COMPANION, Asher Benjamin. The most widely used early 19th century architectural style and source book, for colonial up into Greek Revival periods. Extensive development of geometry of carpentering, construction of sashes, frames, doors, stairs; plans and elevations of domestic and other buildings. Hundreds of thousands of houses were built according to this book, now invaluable to historians, architects, restorers, etc. 1827 edition. 59 plates. 114pp. 7⅞ x 10¾. 22236-5 Paperbound $3.00

DUTCH HOUSES IN THE HUDSON VALLEY BEFORE 1776, Helen Wilkinson Reynolds. The standard survey of the Dutch colonial house and outbuildings, with constructional features, decoration, and local history associated with individual homesteads. Introduction by Franklin D. Roosevelt. Map. 150 illustrations. 469pp. 6⅝ x 9¼. 21469-9 Paperbound $3.50

TWO LITTLE SAVAGES; BEING THE ADVENTURES OF TWO BOYS WHO LIVED AS INDIANS AND WHAT THEY LEARNED, Ernest Thompson Seton. Great classic of nature and boyhood provides a vast range of woodlore in most palatable form, a genuinely entertaining story. Two farm boys build a teepee in woods and live in it for a month, working out Indian solutions to living problems, star lore, birds and animals, plants, etc. 293 illustrations. vii + 286pp.
20985-7 Paperbound $1.95

PETER PIPER'S PRACTICAL PRINCIPLES OF PLAIN & PERFECT PRONUNCIATION. Alliterative jingles and tongue-twisters of surprising charm, that made their first appearance in America about 1830. Republished in full with the spirited woodcut illustrations from this earliest American edition. 32pp. 4½ x 6⅜.
22560-7 Paperbound $1.00

SCIENCE EXPERIMENTS AND AMUSEMENTS FOR CHILDREN, Charles Vivian. 73 easy experiments, requiring only materials found at home or easily available, such as candles, coins, steel wool, etc.; illustrate basic phenomena like vacuum, simple chemical reaction, etc. All safe. Modern, well-planned. Formerly *Science Games for Children.* 102 photos, numerous drawings. 96pp. 6⅛ x 9¼.
21856-2 Paperbound $1.25

AN INTRODUCTION TO CHESS MOVES AND TACTICS SIMPLY EXPLAINED, Leonard Barden. Informal intermediate introduction, quite strong in explaining reasons for moves. Covers basic material, tactics, important openings, traps, positional play in middle game, end game. Attempts to isolate patterns and recurrent configurations. Formerly *Chess.* 58 figures. 102pp. (USO) 21210-6 Paperbound $1.25

LASKER'S MANUAL OF CHESS, Dr. Emanuel Lasker. Lasker was not only one of the five great World Champions, he was also one of the ablest expositors, theorists, and analysts. In many ways, his Manual, permeated with his philosophy of battle, filled with keen insights, is one of the greatest works ever written on chess. Filled with analyzed games by the great players. A single-volume library that will profit almost any chess player, beginner or master. 308 diagrams. xli x 349pp.
20640-8 Paperbound $2.50

THE MASTER BOOK OF MATHEMATICAL RECREATIONS, Fred Schuh. In opinion of many the finest work ever prepared on mathematical puzzles, stunts, recreations; exhaustively thorough explanations of mathematics involved, analysis of effects, citation of puzzles and games. Mathematics involved is elementary. Translated by F. Göbel. 194 figures. xxiv + 430pp. 22134-2 Paperbound $3.00

MATHEMATICS, MAGIC AND MYSTERY, Martin Gardner. Puzzle editor for Scientific American explains mathematics behind various mystifying tricks: card tricks, stage "mind reading," coin and match tricks, counting out games, geometric dissections, etc. Probability sets, theory of numbers clearly explained. Also provides more than 400 tricks, guaranteed to work, that you can do. 135 illustrations. xii + 176pp.
20338-2 Paperbound $1.50

AGAINST THE GRAIN (A REBOURS), Joris K. Huysmans. Filled with weird images, evidences of a bizarre imagination, exotic experiments with hallucinatory drugs, rich tastes and smells and the diversions of its sybarite hero Duc Jean des Esseintes, this classic novel pushed 19th-century literary decadence to its limits. Full unabridged edition. Do not confuse this with abridged editions generally sold. Introduction by Havelock Ellis. xlix + 206pp. 22190-3 Paperbound $2.00

VARIORUM SHAKESPEARE: HAMLET. Edited by Horace H. Furness; a landmark of American scholarship. Exhaustive footnotes and appendices treat all doubtful words and phrases, as well as suggested critical emendations throughout the play's history. First volume contains editor's own text, collated with all Quartos and Folios. Second volume contains full first Quarto, translations of Shakespeare's sources (Belleforest, and Saxo Grammaticus), Der Bestrafte Brudermord, and many essays on critical and historical points of interest by major authorities of past and present. Includes details of staging and costuming over the years. By far the best edition available for serious students of Shakespeare. Total of xx + 905pp.
21004-9, 21005-7, 2 volumes, Paperbound $5.25

A LIFE OF WILLIAM SHAKESPEARE, Sir Sidney Lee. This is the standard life of Shakespeare, summarizing everything known about Shakespeare and his plays. Incredibly rich in material, broad in coverage, clear and judicious, it has served thousands as the best introduction to Shakespeare. 1931 edition. 9 plates. xxix + 792pp. (USO) 21967-4 Paperbound $3.75

MASTERS OF THE DRAMA, John Gassner. Most comprehensive history of the drama in print, covering every tradition from Greeks to modern Europe and America, including India, Far East, etc. Covers more than 800 dramatists, 2000 plays, with biographical material, plot summaries, theatre history, criticism, etc. "Best of its kind in English," *New Republic.* 77 illustrations. xxii + 890pp.
20100-7 Clothbound $7.50

THE EVOLUTION OF THE ENGLISH LANGUAGE, George McKnight. The growth of English, from the 14th century to the present. Unusual, non-technical account presents basic information in very interesting form: sound shifts, change in grammar and syntax, vocabulary growth, similar topics. Abundantly illustrated with quotations. Formerly *Modern English in the Making.* xii + 590pp.
21932-1 Paperbound $3.50

AN ETYMOLOGICAL DICTIONARY OF MODERN ENGLISH, Ernest Weekley. Fullest, richest work of its sort, by foremost British lexicographer. Detailed word histories, including many colloquial and archaic words; extensive quotations. Do not confuse this with the Concise Etymological Dictionary, which is much abridged. Total of xxvii + 830pp. 6½ x 9¼.
21873-2, 21874-0 Two volumes, Paperbound $5.50

FLATLAND: A ROMANCE OF MANY DIMENSIONS, E. A. Abbott. Classic of science-fiction explores ramifications of life in a two-dimensional world, and what happens when a three-dimensional being intrudes. Amusing reading, but also useful as introduction to thought about hyperspace. Introduction by Banesh Hoffmann. 16 illustrations. xx + 103pp. 20001-9 Paperbound $1.00

POEMS OF ANNE BRADSTREET, edited with an introduction by Robert Hutchinson. A new selection of poems by America's first poet and perhaps the first significant woman poet in the English language. 48 poems display her development in works of considerable variety—love poems, domestic poems, religious meditations, formal elegies, "quaternions," etc. Notes, bibliography. viii + 222pp.
22160-1 Paperbound $2.00

THREE GOTHIC NOVELS: THE CASTLE OF OTRANTO BY HORACE WALPOLE; VATHEK BY WILLIAM BECKFORD; THE VAMPYRE BY JOHN POLIDORI, WITH FRAGMENT OF A NOVEL BY LORD BYRON, edited by E. F. Bleiler. The first Gothic novel, by Walpole; the finest Oriental tale in English, by Beckford; powerful Romantic supernatural story in versions by Polidori and Byron. All extremely important in history of literature; all still exciting, packed with supernatural thrills, ghosts, haunted castles, magic, etc. xl + 291pp.
21232-7 Paperbound $2.00

THE BEST TALES OF HOFFMANN, E. T. A. Hoffmann. 10 of Hoffmann's most important stories, in modern re-editings of standard translations: Nutcracker and the King of Mice, Signor Formica, Automata, The Sandman, Rath Krespel, The Golden Flowerpot, Master Martin the Cooper, The Mines of Falun, The King's Betrothed, A New Year's Eve Adventure. 7 illustrations by Hoffmann. Edited by E. F. Bleiler. xxxix + 419pp. 21793-0 Paperbound $2.25

GHOST AND HORROR STORIES OF AMBROSE BIERCE, Ambrose Bierce. 23 strikingly modern stories of the horrors latent in the human mind: The Eyes of the Panther, The Damned Thing, An Occurrence at Owl Creek Bridge, An Inhabitant of Carcosa, etc., plus the dream-essay, Visions of the Night. Edited by E. F. Bleiler. xxii + 199pp. 20767-6 Paperbound $1.50

BEST GHOST STORIES OF J. S. LEFANU, J. Sheridan LeFanu. Finest stories by Victorian master often considered greatest supernatural writer of all. Carmilla, Green Tea, The Haunted Baronet, The Familiar, and 12 others. Most never before available in the U. S. A. Edited by E. F. Bleiler. 8 illustrations from Victorian publications. xvii + 467pp. 20415-4 Paperbound $2.50

THE TIME STREAM, THE GREATEST ADVENTURE, AND THE PURPLE SAPPHIRE—THREE SCIENCE FICTION NOVELS, John Taine (Eric Temple Bell). Great American mathematician was also foremost science fiction novelist of the 1920's. *The Time Stream,* one of all-time classics, uses concepts of circular time; *The Greatest Adventure,* incredibly ancient biological experiments from Antarctica threaten to escape; The *Purple Sapphire,* superscience, lost races in Central Tibet, survivors of the Great Race. 4 illustrations by Frank R. Paul. v + 532pp.
21180-0 Paperbound $2.50

SEVEN SCIENCE FICTION NOVELS, H. G. Wells. The standard collection of the great novels. Complete, unabridged. *First Men in the Moon, Island of Dr. Moreau, War of the Worlds, Food of the Gods, Invisible Man, Time Machine, In the Days of the Comet.* Not only science fiction fans, but every educated person owes it to himself to read these novels. 1015pp. 20264-X Clothbound $5.00

LAST AND FIRST MEN AND STAR MAKER, TWO SCIENCE FICTION NOVELS, Olaf Stapledon. Greatest future histories in science fiction. In the first, human intelligence is the "hero," through strange paths of evolution, interplanetary invasions, incredible technologies, near extinctions and reemergences. Star Maker describes the quest of a band of star rovers for intelligence itself, through time and space: weird inhuman civilizations, crustacean minds, symbiotic worlds, etc. Complete, unabridged. v + 438pp. 21962-3 Paperbound $2.00

THREE PROPHETIC NOVELS, H. G. WELLS. Stages of a consistently planned future for mankind. *When the Sleeper Wakes,* and *A Story of the Days to Come,* anticipate *Brave New World* and *1984,* in the 21st Century; *The Time Machine,* only complete version in print, shows farther future and the end of mankind. All show Wells's greatest gifts as storyteller and novelist. Edited by E. F. Bleiler. x + 335pp. (USO) 20605-X Paperbound $2.00

THE DEVIL'S DICTIONARY, Ambrose Bierce. America's own Oscar Wilde—Ambrose Bierce—offers his barbed iconoclastic wisdom in over 1,000 definitions hailed by H. L. Mencken as "some of the most gorgeous witticisms in the English language." 145pp. 20487-1 Paperbound $1.25

MAX AND MORITZ, Wilhelm Busch. Great children's classic, father of comic strip, of two bad boys, Max and Moritz. Also Ker and Plunk (Plisch und Plumm), Cat and Mouse, Deceitful Henry, Ice-Peter, The Boy and the Pipe, and five other pieces. Original German, with English translation. Edited by H. Arthur Klein; translations by various hands and H. Arthur Klein. vi + 216pp.
20181-3 Paperbound $1.50

PIGS IS PIGS AND OTHER FAVORITES, Ellis Parker Butler. The title story is one of the best humor short stories, as Mike Flannery obfuscates biology and English. Also included, That Pup of Murchison's, The Great American Pie Company, and Perkins of Portland. 14 illustrations. v + 109pp. 21532-6 Paperbound $1.00

THE PETERKIN PAPERS, Lucretia P. Hale. It takes genius to be as stupidly mad as the Peterkins, as they decide to become wise, celebrate the "Fourth," keep a cow, and otherwise strain the resources of the Lady from Philadelphia. Basic book of American humor. 153 illustrations. 219pp. 20794-3 Paperbound $1.25

PERRAULT'S FAIRY TALES, translated by A. E. Johnson and S. R. Littlewood, with 34 full-page illustrations by Gustave Doré. All the original Perrault stories—Cinderella, Sleeping Beauty, Bluebeard, Little Red Riding Hood, Puss in Boots, Tom Thumb, etc.—with their witty verse morals and the magnificent illustrations of Doré. One of the five or six great books of European fairy tales. viii + 117pp. $8\frac{1}{8}$ x 11. 22311-6 Paperbound $2.00

OLD HUNGARIAN FAIRY TALES, Baroness Orczy. Favorites translated and adapted by author of the *Scarlet Pimpernel.* Eight fairy tales include "The Suitors of Princess Fire-Fly," "The Twin Hunchbacks," "Mr. Cuttlefish's Love Story," and "The Enchanted Cat." This little volume of magic and adventure will captivate children as it has for generations. 90 drawings by Montagu Barstow. 96pp.
(USO) 22293-4 Paperbound $1.95

MATHEMATICAL PUZZLES FOR BEGINNERS AND ENTHUSIASTS, Geoffrey Mott-Smith. 189 puzzles from easy to difficult—involving arithmetic, logic, algebra, properties of digits, probability, etc.—for enjoyment and mental stimulus. Explanation of mathematical principles behind the puzzles. 135 illustrations. viii + 248pp.
20198-8 Paperbound $1.25

PAPER FOLDING FOR BEGINNERS, William D. Murray and Francis J. Rigney. Easiest book on the market, clearest instructions on making interesting, beautiful origami. Sail boats, cups, roosters, frogs that move legs, bonbon boxes, standing birds, etc. 40 projects; more than 275 diagrams and photographs. 94pp.
20713-7 Paperbound $1.00

TRICKS AND GAMES ON THE POOL TABLE, Fred Herrmann. 79 tricks and games—some solitaires, some for two or more players, some competitive games—to entertain you between formal games. Mystifying shots and throws, unusual caroms, tricks involving such props as cork, coins, a hat, etc. Formerly *Fun on the Pool Table.* 77 figures. 95pp. 21814-7 Paperbound $1.00

HAND SHADOWS TO BE THROWN UPON THE WALL: A SERIES OF NOVEL AND AMUSING FIGURES FORMED BY THE HAND, Henry Bursill. Delightful picturebook from great-grandfather's day shows how to make 18 different hand shadows: a bird that flies, duck that quacks, dog that wags his tail, camel, goose, deer, boy, turtle, etc. Only book of its sort. vi + 33pp. 6½ x 9¼. 21779-5 Paperbound $1.00

WHITTLING AND WOODCARVING, E. J. Tangerman. 18th printing of best book on market. "If you can cut a potato you can carve" toys and puzzles, chains, chessmen, caricatures, masks, frames, woodcut blocks, surface patterns, much more. Information on tools, woods, techniques. Also goes into serious wood sculpture from Middle Ages to present, East and West. 464 photos, figures. x + 293pp.
20965-2 Paperbound $2.00

HISTORY OF PHILOSOPHY, Julián Marias. Possibly the clearest, most easily followed, best planned, most useful one-volume history of philosophy on the market; neither skimpy nor overfull. Full details on system of every major philosopher and dozens of less important thinkers from pre-Socratics up to Existentialism and later. Strong on many European figures usually omitted. Has gone through dozens of editions in Europe. 1966 edition, translated by Stanley Appelbaum and Clarence Strowbridge. xviii + 505pp. 21739-6 Paperbound $2.75

YOGA: A SCIENTIFIC EVALUATION, Kovoor T. Behanan. Scientific but non-technical study of physiological results of yoga exercises; done under auspices of Yale U. Relations to Indian thought, to psychoanalysis, etc. 16 photos. xxiii + 270pp.
20505-3 Paperbound $2.50

Prices subject to change without notice.
Available at your book dealer or write for free catalogue to Dept. GI, Dover Publications, Inc., 180 Varick St., N. Y., N. Y. 10014. Dover publishes more than 150 books each year on science, elementary and advanced mathematics, biology, music, art, literary history, social sciences and other areas.